# Illegal

# Illegal

✦

## NAFTA refugees forced to flee

*Peter A. Geniesse*

iUniverse, Inc.
New York   Bloomington

**Illegal**
**NAFTA refugees forced to flee**

*iUniverse books may be ordered through booksellers or by contacting:*

*iUniverse*
*1663 Liberty Drive*
*Bloomington, IN 47403*
*www.iuniverse.com*
*1-800-Authors (1-800-288-4677)*

*Because of the dynamic nature of the Internet, any Web addresses or links contained in this book may have changed since publication and may no longer be valid.*

*ISBN: 978-1-4401-9098-8 (sc)*
*ISBN: 978-1-4401-9103-9 (ebk)*

*Printed in the United States of America*

*iUniverse rev. date: 1/21/2009*

***To Antonio and Santiago:***

*May the generation of my grandsons
come to a greater understanding
of the value of immigrants
and the full meaning of
"liberty and justice for all."*

# Contents

# *Preface*

I knew very little about immigration just a dozen years or so ago. Oh, my great-grandparents came over from Belgium back in the 1870s. They settled with their kinfolk in Wisconsin, and farmed hardscrabble lands in Door County, now known as the Cape Cod of the Midwest and Chicago's vacationland.

I never knew those immigrants. I knew their grandchildren, however. They spoke English without accent, went on to college, moved into the cities and made lots of money behind a desk. Some of them married the grandkids of Irish immigrants.

But that's another story.

I did get to know a number of refugees, however. My wife and I helped sponsor a Vietnamese family of seven back in 1981. They were boat people who fled the communist regime after the Vietnam War. Some of them had survived the Killing Fields of Cambodia. I wrote a book about their experiences: *"Cuc: Flower of the Delta."*

As newspaper reporter and editor, I wrote lots of pieces about the Vietnamese, as well as the Hmong refugees from Laos. Thousands of Hmong moved from the United Nations' refugee camps in Thailand to Northeastern Wisconsin in the late 1970s and early 1980s. They had fled their homelands in the wake of the Vietnam War. They were our allies, their lives were in danger and we gave them haven.

It was a most difficult transition both for them and for the community. And it was not without incidents of racism and discrimination. They spoke their native languages, settled in clusters and retained their customs. The distinct Hmong culture made it ever more difficult for their elders to assimilate into society.

But their children did. Most now speak English quite well, and many are college-educated citizens who have become full contributing members of American society.

By the time the millions of Vietnamese and Hmong were successfully resettled in the U.S., another ethnic group was about to cross U.S. borders.

Most spoke Spanish, most were Mexicans and most were illegal. They had no visas, but they were desperate and they came to work.

They were forced to migrate from their homelands, not because of war, but because of U.S. economic policies. They were NAFTA refugees. The U.S. government called them "illegal aliens," and set out, not to welcome them, but to deport them and fence out the next wave of immigrants.

There's a big difference between being a refugee and an immigrant, especially one without documents. Refugees don't have to hide in the shadows, ever fearful of being deported. They have government support. They have rights. Immigrants have rights, too, but they're most often trampled without impunity.

Two decades ago, there were lots of refugees but very few new immigrants in Northeastern Wisconsin. Milwaukee long had enclaves of Hispanics but most of the rest of the state recognized Latinos as migrant workers who followed the crop harvests. Most of them returned to Texas before winter set in.

I sometimes overheard Spanish conversation in the supermarkets, but Latinos weren't prominent in public.

Late one night in early January of 2000, I got a call from the local Red Cross office, asking me to help out at an apartment fire. I was a member of the board, the only one who could speak Spanish, and I was told that many Hispanics lived there.

When I arrived at the scene, flames were shooting out the roof of the two-story, 40-unit building. I recognized the site. I had lived there 30 years earlier when the frame structure had seen better times.

The temperature was 10-below and wind gusts fanned the flames, hampering the firefighters' efforts. The parking lot was a sheet of ice. There were a number of cars there, clunkers, with their engines running. Upon closer inspection, there were lots of people, kids and babies, too, wrapped in blankets and huddled in those vehicles. They were silent and scared.

The Red Cross had set up an emergency shelter in a nearby Appleton elementary school that was still on Christmas vacation. There were cots and blankets, and clothes and hot food available. We were equipped to handle more than 100 people. My task was to convince them to come.

I tapped on the car windows, but the drivers just stared ahead. I yelled in Spanish that I was from the Red Cross, that we had available housing and food for their families, and everything was free. I insisted that the Red Cross had nothing to do with the government, that it didn't matter whether they had legal documents or not.

At least 100 people, almost all Hispanics, lived in the apartments, including several families who had occupied the basement storage areas. Only

30 came to the emergency shelter that night. The others remained in their cars, with the motors running. They had lost all their belongings in the fire. But they feared being discovered, jailed and deported. They couldn't trust anyone.

Over the course of the following week, a few showed up at the emergency shelter as word spread that the Red Cross was friend not foe. Little by little, they began to trust me and related poignant immigrant stories. Most were from Mexico, although a few were from Guatemala, Nicaragua and Honduras. All were undocumented. All were employed, some holding two menial jobs. Some had been cheated by employers, but they had no recourse.

In the aftermath of the apartment fire, when the daily newspaper pointed out that most of the residents were undocumented Latinos, the community was shocked. Most had no idea there were illegal aliens in our midst. As a newspaperman, I should have known.

The image of toddlers with sad eyes and frightened families who had lost all their belongings in a fire, whose only refuge on a bone-chilling night was an old rusty vehicle, stayed with me for a long time.

These weren't criminals. They were desperate people. Who would leave his homeland and his kinfolk to come to the frozen north, to live in the shadows ever fearful of being arrested and deported? Who would risk his life and that of his children to cross deserts, mountains and rivers in the pursuit of a menial job? Who would want to be demonized and held in contempt by his new community?

Just why did millions of Mexicans and other Hispanics come to the U.S. in droves? Why now?

Those questions spurred my quest to discover the real roots of migration. They led me to join an interfaith justice group called ESTHER, part of the Gamaliel Foundation, that was focusing on the immigration issue. I befriended dozens of Hispanics, taught many of them English and even conducted U.S. citizenship classes.

Still, I was stunned at the turnout when the Mexican consulate officials from Chicago came to Appleton to issue identification cards to its citizens living in exile. More than one thousand Mexicans, almost all undocumented, registered one year, and 1,500 the next. In a matter of just a couple of years, the Hispanic population in Wisconsin's Fox Valley had grown to more than 10,000. Now to Texas and Arizona and California and even to Chicago, that's not a big number. But to Northeastern Wisconsin, it's substantial.

I was still in search of the root cause of migration when I joined a Witness for Peace delegation to Oaxaca, Mexico, in early 2009. The group was from North Carolina and members stayed with families in a mountaintop indigenous village. Most of the families sent sons and daughters to North Carolina to work in the fields when their own agricultural economy collapsed.

Next, I needed to know how they crossed the border. I had visited most of the Texas frontier cities, and had seen migrant families crossing the Rio Grande only to be detained on the other side by the Border Patrol. But I knew little of the perils of the Sonora desert. So I joined another Witness for Peace delegation at the Altar crossroads, the staging area for thousands of migrants who each day trek over mountains and through unforgiving deserts to make it to America.

Then, I capped that experience with a solidarity march of more than seven miles along the migrant trail in 115-degree temperatures. We had water and food and escorts. The migrants don't.

I now have a lot more insights about immigration than I did just 12 years ago. And hopefully after reading this book, you will too.

# A LOS CAIDOS EN LOS DESIERTOS DE LA MUERTE

*To the Fallen in the Deserts of Death.*

**En memoria de aquellos que por buscar una mejor vida,**
*In memory of those who in search of a better life,*
**Lo único que encontaron fue la muerte,**
*The only thing they found was death,*
**En recuerdo de aquellos que todo los arriesgaron y todo lo perdieron.**
*In remembrance of those who risked everything and lost everything.*
**Se fueron con la esperanza en los ojos**
*Those who went with hope in their eyes*
**Y el desafío en el alma.**
*And challenge in their souls.*

**Somos un grito que demanda justicia,**
*We are a cry that demands justice,*
**Para que nadie nunca más tenga que abandonar su tierra,**
*So that no one ever has to leave his land,*
**Sus creencias, sus muertos, sus hijos, sus padres, su familia,**
*His beliefs, his deceased, his children, his parents, his family*
**Sus raices, su cultura, su identidad.**
*His roots, his culture, his identity.*

**Somos un silencio que se hace voz**
*We are the silence that has a voice*
**Para que nadie tenga que ir a buscar un destino en otras tierras,**
*So that no one has to go to seek his destiny in other lands,*
**Para que nadie tenga que ir al destierro**
*So that no one has to go into exile*
**Y consumirse en soledad.**
*And waste away in solitude.*

**Somos una voz que el desierto no puede ahogar,**
*We are a voice in the desert that can't be stifled*
**Para exigir que la patria les dé por igual a todos sus hijos**
*To demand that our nation give all its children*
**La oportunidad de una vida digna y decorosa.**
*The opportunity to have a life of dignity and respect..*

*"Por el derecho a vivir en paz," written by Othón Pérez, 2004,*
*is engraved at the entrance to Casa de Migrante,*
*Altar, Sonora, Mexico,*
*where tens of thousands of migrants have gathered before*
*embarking on the perilous journey to the U.S. across the Sonoran Desert.*

# Introduction

"When the U.S. catches a cold, Mexico gets pneumonia."

That's what they used to say about the dependant relationship of the highly disparate neighbors. But in today's global society, it sometimes goes both ways.

The world is interconnected like never before. Take the swine flu pandemic, for example. Mexico was the incubator in the spring of 2009 but the United States soon outpaced its neighbor in the number of cases. And in a matter of weeks, the bug had infected the world.

The suspected source was an industrial pig farm, operated by an American company under lax NAFTA rules, in a tiny village in the Mexican state of Veracruz. It could have happened anywhere on the globe. But a five-year-old boy named Edgar Hernández in a hamlet called La Gloria triggered the panic button on April 3, 2009.

Smithfield Foods, the world's largest pork producer, operated a massive factory farm upwind from La Gloria that delivered 950,000 hogs a year to market. Villagers had long complained of the stench that wafted their way from the open manure tanks. Some insisted it made them sick, but Edgar, who recovered rather quickly, was the first to be diagnosed. La Gloria, with no other claim to fame, decided to put up a statue in his honor.

The swine flu story in early October of 2009 began another chapter under the title of H1N1. Mexico recorded almost 500 cases in one day, and the United States and the world nervously awaited the strain to spread. Millions of doses of vaccines have been rushed to clinics across the U.S. While health care for the undocumented is a hot button topic, when it comes to swine flu the U.S. government has waived the rules. The 12 million illegal aliens are being offered the shots with no questions asked.

It's an increasingly small world, with the chasm growing ever greater between the haves and the have-nots. This has forced countless millions of poor people to set out on a journey away from their homelands in search of the means to feed their families. The age of migration is a worldwide phenomenon with an estimated 200 million people on the go. Many are refugees, others are internally displaced, but perhaps 40 million migrants are without legal documents.

About one-third of the world's undocumented live and work in the U.S. The vast majority are Hispanics, and most of those are Mexicans. About 11% of everyone born in Mexico is currently living in the U.S. That's 12.7 million Mexican immigrants, and 55% of those don't have legal papers.

The Mexican migration is the largest flow of people in the world. No other country has as many total immigrants from all countries as the U.S. has immigrants from Mexico alone. One-third of all foreign-born people in the U.S. are from Mexico.

As late as 1960, Mexico ranked seventh as a source of immigrants to the U.S., behind Italy, Germany, Canada, the Soviet Union, the United Kingdom and Poland. By 1980, Mexico was No. 1. Its numbers doubled in that decade and more than doubled again between 1990 and 2000.

The numbers beg the question: why? There have been no wars, nor famine, nor major calamities in Mexico during the past three decades. The Germans and the Irish dominated the flood of immigrants in the late 19th century due to those causes. The massive surge of Mexican immigrants was brought about by a sudden increase in poverty. But what caused that? Why were there so relatively few Mexicans in America in 1970 and three decades later there were 17 times as many?

The answer is found in the root causes of migration. Few are fond of tracing those roots; many prefer to decry and deport the legions who are in the U.S. illegally. But if they took a closer look, they'd see that the United States government is to blame in large part for the immigration imbroglio that now faces the nation.

The often stormy relationship between the big brother up north and the little brother down south goes back more than 160 years. The U.S. sent troops to Mexico City to get its way, and then annexed one third of the country's territory. Mexicans didn't like it but they got over it. What could they do? It was America's manifest destiny.

On more than one occasion, the U.S. has acted more like big bully than big brother.

For the next century, the U.S. cast a giant shadow over its reticent kin. There were alternate periods of benign neglect and hostility, along with measures of cooperation where the U.S. would set the rules. When the U.S. needed Mexicans to harvest the crops during both World War I and World War II, millions got permits. When their services were no longer needed, they got deported.

The *Bracero* program, which employed generations of Mexicans until the mid-1960s, became a family tradition in some locations. When the program was eliminated, many continued to work in the U.S. for at least half the year. They had no legal papers, but it didn't seem to matter. In fact, many employers were OK with illegal aliens. They could pay them less and no one could complain.

There really was no fuss over illegal immigration until the big surge of the 1980s.

Mexico, awash with newfound oil, went deep in debt, counting on Pemex's inflated profits to bail out the country. But in 1982, the world price of oil collapsed, and Mexico defaulted on its debt payments to U.S. and European banks.

To the rescue came the International Monetary Fund and the World Bank, agencies controlled by the U.S. and a handful of other First World nations. To get out of debt, the agencies laid out "Structural Adjustment Programs" that Mexico had to follow to be attractive to foreign investors.

These included privatizing national industries, cutting public services, removing wage and price protection, eliminating tariffs and barriers to trade and devaluing its currency to stimulate exports. It was called "neo-liberalism," or *laissez faire* in another era. It aimed to please its suitors at the expense of its people.

Large-scale export agriculture was to replace staple foods farms. Jobs and wages were slashed, food subsidies were ended and the national currency was devalued. The cost of living soared. The minimum wage went up 136% in the 1980s but the cost of a basket of basic goods soared by 371%. The jobless rate hit 15%, but a more telling statistic, underemployment, involved another 40% of the people.

By 1990, more than half of all Mexicans lived in poverty. More than 18 million lived in conditions of extreme poverty.

After a decade of abiding by the terms of the Structural Adjustment Program, Mexico's rich had become ever richer, and its poor, ever so much more desperate, left the land and headed north.

And then came NAFTA and much more of the same.

The North American Free Trade Agreement, forged by three unequal partners, went into effect on New Year's Day in 1994. The U.S. heralded it as the world's largest free trade area, encompassing 439 million people producing $15.3 trillion worth of goods and services annually.

NAFTA got off to a rocky start. Free trade and foreign investment was supposed to pave the way for Mexico to enter the First World. By the end of the year, the peso sank from three to ten to the dollar, panicked investors pulled out their money and the Mexican meltdown was underway. The jobless rate doubled, inflation hit 50%, and millions of Mexicans crossed the northern frontier.

NAFTA promised a more prosperous Mexico that would "export goods, not people." Fifteen years later, more than 10 million Mexicans have fled the country. Two million of them were farmers who were put out of business by unfair trade. They couldn't compete with the highly efficient and highly subsidized U.S. corporate agriculture.

NAFTA rules eliminated subsidies for Mexican farmers and price controls for consumers. But the U.S. didn't have to play by the same rules. The U.S.

subsidizes its corn farmers alone to the tune of $10 billion a year. Mexico's total agricultural budget is less than $1 billion.

Such are the disparities between NAFTA neighbors.

While millions of undocumented Mexicans had crossed the U.S. border by the turn of the century, it took the 9-11 terrorist attack to bring the immigration issue to the forefront. Suddenly it became a matter of national security.

The U.S. spent billions and billions of dollars to corral the flood of migrants, many of them children of *Braceros* who worked legally in America for more than two decades. Some 700 miles of frontier fences were installed, the U.S. Border Patrol numbers were doubled, detention facilities to hold thousands were constructed, and the Department of Homeland Security and its Immigration and Customs Enforcement agency (ICE) were bolstered to meet the terrorism threat.

Their efforts nabbed millions of migrants, but no known terrorists.

The Mexican government certainly hasn't embraced the immigration enforcement tactics. But it's careful not to protest too loudly. After all, some 21 million North Americans spend a lot of money at Cancun and other tourist haunts each year. Hundreds of U.S. companies employ more than one million Mexicans in *maquiladora* industries on the border. And millions of Mexicans working in the U.S. send back a couple of billion dollars to their families and communities. Remittances are Mexico's second largest source of revenue, next to oil.

And then there's a matter of occasional money orders from Uncle Sam. President Clinton forwarded $2.5 billion in loans with a 10-year payback from America's "friends" account to help rescue Mexico from its currency crisis of 1995. He had proposed a $40 billion bailout, but the U.S. Congress balked at the idea.

Not long afterwards, the U.S. routinely provided $112 million for training, arms and equipment for Mexico's military.

There was something called Plan Puebla Panama, and $50 billion of infrastructure projects intended to link Central America to the southern Mexican states in a Free Trade Area of the Americas. One key project involved power transmission lines from Mexico to Panama with the goal of providing electricity generated in the region to the U.S. The scheme was shelved, but it still could be resurrected as part of "Plan Mesoamerica."

Then there's the current $1.6 billion "Mérida Initiative," commonly called "Plan Mexico," aimed to curb the drug wars that have slain thousands and sent billions of dollars worth of cocaine, marijuana and even heroin to the U.S., the world's largest market for illicit drugs. Ninety percent of the drugs go to the U.S. and 90% of the weapons used in the killings by Mexico's drug cartels come from the U.S.

The three-year plan amounts to a ten-fold increase in U.S. military aid to Mexico, and includes helicopters, patrol planes and surveillance equipment, all purchased from U.S. contractors.

The United States has long exerted its influence in Mexico's affairs via dollar diplomacy. Much of it has been overt and some of it quite heavy handed. But there have been occasions when U.S. meddling has come to light only many years later.

The 1968 Olympics in Mexico City continues to carry the student massacre stigma. The Mexican military gunned down 300 protesters in the Plaza de Tres Culturas on Oct. 2. Recent investigations revealed the CIA, fearing the riots would disrupt the games 10 days later, had been monitoring the situation. The U.S. sent in weapons, ammunition and riot control equipment before and during the crisis.

The birthday of NAFTA in 1994 was greeted by protests in the indigenous state of Chiapas where the Zapatistas, an armed coalition of Mayan Indians, took control of several communities on New Year's Day to send a message to Mexico City and the world. The next day Mexico sent in thousands of troops to crush the uprising, resulting in the deaths of 145 people.

Only later was it revealed that Mexican officials had received a message from a New York bank "to get rid of the Zapatistas" in exchange for full bailout financing, promised by President Clinton.

The Bush National Security Doctrine of 2002 was seen as the greatest expression of U.S. hegemony since the Monroe Doctrine. Four years later it led to the "Security and Prosperity Partnership," the armoring of NAFTA.

The "Three Amigos," Presidents George W. Bush and Vincente Fox and Prime Minister Paul Martin signed on to the plan that left no doubt who was at the helm of the hemisphere.

The U.S. had created a plan to protect the "shared economic space" and pushed the borders of its security perimeter beyond its frontiers to include Mexico and Canada.

The SPP provisions were aimed to remove barriers to the flow of capital and cross-border production. They also were intended to secure access to natural resources in the two countries, notably oil.

"The prosperity of the United States," the document stated, "relies heavily on a secure supply of imported energy."

It was a stark reminder to its neighbors that what was good for the United States, was good for North America, if not the world.

TIJUANA

NOGALES

C. JUAREZ

United States

LAREDO

*Rio Grande*

REYNOSA

GULF OF CALIFORNIA

United States
of Mexico

GULF
OF
MEXICO

LOS CABOS

MATAMOROS

MAZATLAN

MONTERREY

PACIFIC OCEAN

P. VALLARTA

TAMPICO

GUANAJUATO

CANCUN

GUADALAJARA

VERACRUZ

★ MEXICO CITY

ACAPULCO

OAXACA

CHIAPAS

**Map by David A. Wollangk**

# Chapter One

## *Tourism -1*

✦

### *An American in Mexico: It sure isn't the 1960s*

For nearly a half-century, I've savored the Mexican tourist scene. I've visited nearly every state, every border town, every colonial gem, and just about every pyramid and Mayan ruin. And yes, I've been to the beach and most of the planned seaside vacation resorts. I've lost count of how many times I've been to Mexico, but it must be a score or more.

Things have changed, of course. It's not your grandpa's Mexico. The country has changed. The people have changed. And so have the tourists.

I studied Spanish in Cuernavaca back in the early 1960s, and I fell in love with the country. Those were the days when I'd grab my backpack and hop on a third class bus and go wherever it was going. I'd eat on the street or in the markets where I could buy a fresh bolillo and a ripe avocado for a nickel and make a meal out of it. I'd stroll the dusty streets alone and I'd stay in a dingy hotel room in a forgotten town for a dollar or so.

And I was never afraid.

I was greeted by warm smiles wherever I trekked. Some would shake their heads at the crazy gringo, but everyone I met welcomed me into their community. A friendly, hospitable people, the likes I haven't seen since.

Once I was the weekend guest of a super-rich family in Mexico City that was in the midst of celebrating a *"quinciñera"* for their 15-year-old daughter at a five-star hotel. I also was invited to stay at their villa in Cuernavaca, a mansion with a pool and flower gardens and lots of servants, all hidden by a wall covered with bougainvilleas.

Once I spent the night in a scrap tin shack with a mud floor in the midst of a vast Mexico City slum, sharing space with a family of five, along with two turkeys and a pig. There was no electricity or running water and the two-

1

hole outhouse also accommodated the neighbors. The next morning I was served two fried eggs, beans and tortillas while the three young children, with hunger in their eyes, sat silently alongside me on the dirt floor. I was a guest, their parents said. There wasn't enough food to go around that day.

I really learned to love Mexico City, with all its bustle, its monuments, museums and parks and festivals. I looked forward to going to the bullfights at Plaza Mexico on Sundays afternoons, and shouting olé in chorus with the masses and sharing a squirt of wine from a skin that was tossed about the sunny side crowds.

I was a regular at Caldo de Pollo, a chicken soup stand hidden in an alley behind the Revolution Monument at the base of the Avenida Juárez. The five-table eatery featured a steaming bowl of broth, garbanzo beans, sprigs of cilantro and a huge chunk of chicken breast. Once they ran out of *"pechuga"* but begged me to stick around while they searched for some. As I downed another Modelo, a weathered man in overalls stepped in the door and carried two live chickens over his shoulder into the kitchen. The waiter delivered a hot stack of tortillas and another beer *"gratis"* and announced that my soup would be right out.

Tears welled in my eyes as I witnessed the devastation from the 1985 earthquake that reduced stately hotels and centuries-old buildings in the heart of Mexico City's historic Alameda to rubble. It was an 8.1 magnitude quake that killed 10,000 and destroyed 500 major buildings, including 13 hospitals. I was at the Mexico City airport, between flights to Nicaragua, a year after the quake. I hired a taxi to survey the scene, and to see if Caldo de Pollo was still standing. It was.

Once on a motor trip through Mexico, our new station wagon developed transmission problems. Actually the flaw was discovered soon after leaving Wisconsin. The car was under warranty and by the time we got to Laredo, Texas, we had stopped at four dealer garages for repairs. Two just added fluid and sent us on our way. Two did major surgery, with expensive parts. None sought to really diagnose the problem.

Except for a single stall garage on the outskirts of Veracruz. When I explained to the mechanic all the repairs that had been done in the U.S., he said simply, "Señor, we don't have any parts. But I will fix your car." He laid down on his back in the grease pit and had me drive the car back and forth over him. Then he pulled a thread from his torn jeans, dabbed it with glue and wound it around the errant screw, cause of the transmission leak. "It's fixed," he declared. "No charge."

Back in the 1960s, there was little fear in driving about Mexico, except perhaps for Mexico City and its monumental round-abouts, narrow side streets and crazy taxicab drivers. Early one Sunday morning, I had pulled up for a stop sign in the left lane on a one-way street when a yellow taxi burst past me on the right and whipped a left in front of my car. I nicked his bumper. The driver and his passenger ganged up on me, saying that since I hit the taxi, it was my fault.

They were willing to settle for $100. Then $50. Then $10. *Nada, nunca,* I insisted, using some choice Spanish expressions. Let's call in a cop, I said. The officer ruled it was my fault, but I could plead my case in front of a magistrate, he said. The court wouldn't be in session for another six hours. It's OK with me, I said. The driver said no, he couldn't afford to lose six hours of fares.

His passenger smiled and held out his hand. "Congratulations, gringo, you won the game." The driver, too, shook my hand, and waved as he drove off. And yes, I discovered, it was my fault under Mexican law. It didn't matter that the taxi ran a stop sign and cut me off with a reckless left turn. He who hits, pays.

I've visited all parts of Mexico, from Chihuahua to Chiapas, by car and by bus and by plane. Once a pilot friend and I flew a single-engine Cessna from Wisconsin to Mexico City, and then ventured across the Gulf of Cortéz to remote fishing villages in Baja California.

My wife Jill and I honeymooned in Mexico, visiting both Acapulco and a fledgling resort called Puerto Vallarta, best known at the time as Elizabeth Taylor and Richard Burton's romantic hideway. We later returned to spend the night at Mismaloya, the abandoned movie set for "Night of the Iguana."

We climbed the snow-capped, volcanic peak of Popocatépetl, although we stopped short of the 17,000-foot summit on the day of a total solar eclipse. We drove to San Cristóbol de las Casas in the mountains of Chiapas, and to an indigenous enclave not far from the Guatemalan border. We stayed almost a month at San Blas, Nayarit, the historic village from where Father Junípero Serra set out to establish and supply 21 California missions.

We befriended a poor Mexican boy who was barred from the church procession on the feast of San Blas because he didn't have a candle. We gave him ours. The word spread fast and we were soon surrounded by the poor, kids and adults. The boy's mother asked us to be his *padrinos* for confirmation. We accepted the offer.

These experiences were from another era. They were before Cancun, and before burgeoning populations, and such things as NAFTA and drug cartels. The world has changed over the last four decades. And although there likely are a few remote areas of Mexico where hospitality and friendliness still reign, to a tourist who roamed free of care in the 1960s, Mexico is just not the same place.

In the early 1960s. Mexico had a population of 25 million. That's the whole country. Mexico City has that many people today. Over the past four decades, the country's population has soared to more than 100 million. That has been translated into fewer small towns and a lot more crowded urban areas.

By the mid-1970s, Mexican tourism would be changed forever. Instead of appealing to well-heeled Americans on one end and Volkswagen bus beachcombers on the other, Mexico set out to create from scratch a megaresort for middleclass Americans who could dine at McDonalds, drink the water and never have to speak Spanish.

Cancun was the first and is still Mexico's largest planned resort complex. It was highly successful from the start and it set the stage for other planned Pacific coastal resorts such as Puerto Vallarta, Ixtapa, Los Cabos and Huatulco. Villages were created apart from the resorts to house job seekers. No more could tourists and workers rub shoulders after hours.

The beach was the drawing card. Sunny, warm days welcomed the winter guests from the north. Mexico's mystique, as well as its archeological and cultural riches, now came in a distant second place.

Mexico enjoyed the tourist boom of the 1980s, and the government was about to embrace the economic promises of the North American Free Trade Agreement (NAFTA) when it received a stunning wake-up call from its indigenous citizens.

It was New Year's Day, 1994, the day when NAFTA was to go into effect. Bands of armed Indians took over four remote towns and the Chiapas mountain capital of San Cristóbol de las Casas. Once again the indigenous had been left out of the Mexico's new economic equation, and they were making a political statement. The government responded by sending in the troops.

To the outside world, the demands weren't taken seriously. A masked, charismatic leader called Subcomandante Marcos led the Zapatistas, named for the famed peasant revolutionary, Emiliano Zapata.

Many said Mexico didn't have a racial problem. A number of national heroes were pure-blooded Indians, and so were lots of elected officials, including a president, Benito Juárez, a Zapotec Indian from Oaxaca. Most Mexicans are mestizos (Spanish-Indian), but about 30% are considered indigenous.

The Zapatista uprising in the southernmost state, the poorest and most indigenous, triggered national turmoil that put Chiapas on the world map.

Twenty years earlier, my wife and I had found San Cristóbol a peaceful, delightful sanctuary. The pine-clad mountains that tumble down to the

Lacandón rainforest and jungles that hid Palenque's Mayan treasures were truly awesome.

But this time the situation was tense, dangerous, actually. We had entered an armed camp after a short bus ride from a resort in Huatulco. Mexican soldiers manned machine gun bunkers and checkpoints surrounding the city. They boarded the buses, checked IDs and searched for weapons.

We stayed at a "safe house" called Na Bolom, established by a Swiss anthropologist and Danish archeologist couple who promoted and protected the Lacandón Indians. The other safe house in San Cristoból was the centuries-old Catholic cathedral, presided over by Bishop Samuel Ruíz, once a nominee for the Nobel Peace Prize.

The bishop was a staunch defender of Indian rights. He also was branded as a leftist and labeled "Obispo Rojo." He brushed aside such criticism. He was following in the footsteps of San Cristobol's first bishop, Bartolemé de Las Casas, back in 1544.

Bishop Ruíz had received numerous death threats for his support of the Zapatista cause. He was unfazed. He called on fellow Latin American bishops to attend a solidarity rally in the cathedral. They filled the sanctuary. My wife and I were in a middle pew. Soldiers armed with automatic weapons surrounded the *zócalo*. It was a tense time. Then the massive doors of the ancient cathedral opened and in processed Bishop Ruíz, closely flanked by more than 100 bodyguards, Tzotzils and Tzeltals, Maya tribal descendants.

There were relatively few casualties officially reported in the three-year standoff between the Zapatistas and the Mexican military. Negotiations finally ended the siege, and Indians throughout the country benefited from the political, social and economic concessions.

However, the Zapatistas didn't get what they wanted most that fateful New Year's Day: the re-negotiation of NAFTA.

Meanwhile, back along the Pacific away from the fray, tourism was on the rebound. Condos were sprouting up along the shores and coastal ridges. As the money rolled in from the resorts, it attracted some unsavory investors. Time-share pitches and giveaways were everywhere. My wife and I succumbed to an offer we couldn't refuse: a week just off the beach in Mazatlan for 30 years for $1,200. That price included a week's stay bonus, a $50 meal coupon, along with a bottle of Kahlua and a blanket.

Now, it wasn't a five-star hotel. But it was comfortable and convenient and the manager pledged within the year to renovate the place, expand the swimming pool and build a hot tub and a recreational deck. The following year when we arrived to spend our week, the bags of cement and re-bars were still piled at the entrance.

I asked to see the manager. He's not with us, I was told. Where is he? He's dead. How did he die? He was shot to death. Who did it? The drug cartel. Where did it happen?  Right here in the lobby. You can still see the bullet holes in the wall. Why? He held out on the money due the Sinaloa cartel. Did anyone see who fired the AK-47? I was behind the desk that day, but no, I sure didn't see anyone.

Don't worry, the clerk said. You're safe here. They're only killing their rivals.

The year was 1995, and the drug cartels already were firmly entrenched in the country.

A dozen years later, my wife and I were standing in Reynosa's crowded city square on a Sunday afternoon carrying a large black suitcase.  It was a festive occasion and families filled the *zócolo*. We had taken a taxi across the border from McAllen, Texas, and were awaiting the arrival of a Mexican friend to deliver some clothes and some gifts for his family, including a doll for his daughter.

Our friend was later than usual, and our presence and our suitcase stirred unusual interest. Several cars paused at the street corner across from the cathedral, and one man sidled up to us, nodding toward the suitcase, and when we didn't respond he jumped into a passing car.

It all might have been innocent enough. But it was unnerving, a bit scary. It became downright frightening when we read of the surge in crime, kidnapping, murder and drug cartel violence in Reynosa in a Texas newspaper the next day.

The spiraling violence has led to a sharp downturn in tourism, especially on the  U.S. frontier. Tijuana reportedly has shown a drop of up to 70% in tourism dollars in 2008. Nogales, Arizona, residents no longer feel safe to visit relatives in their sister city across the border in the wake of recent shootings and grenade attacks.

Border city mayors and business leaders insist that the violence involves only drug cartels and other criminals and is not directed at visitors.

Still, it's scary. When you cross a Rio Grande bridge and enter Mexico you now are greeted by a cluster of military vehicles with mounted machine guns, and a company of soldiers with stern faces and bullet-proof vests, cradling automatic weapons.

For tourists, it's not what you'd call a warm, friendly welcome.

# Chapter One

## *Tourism -2*

✦

### *One million Americans now call Mexico home*

Millions of North Americans flood across the Mexican frontier each year, unfettered by towering fences, border guards and visa restrictions.

They need only an ID, a driver's license and more recently a passport, along with a wallet filled with cash, credit and ATM cards to be warmly welcomed.

Of course, it's not the same story for Mexicans trying to get into the United States.

There are now nearly one million expatriates from the U.S. who have taken up residence in Mexico. Most are retirees. Some are snowbirds, some are year-rounders; some own fancy villas, some live in modest rental units. Many have been settled in the sun for decades and rarely return to the U.S.

Millions more Americans – and Canadians too -- regularly visit coastal Mexican resorts. And then there are American businesses and industries, not just inside the frontier fences but throughout the country. Add conventioneers, spring break college kids, border hoppers and Spanish language learners and Mexico is full of gringos of all ages at all times.

A total of 21.4 million people visited Mexico in 2006. They spent $12.1 billion.

Tourism is, indeed, a huge industry. Mexico is the number one destination for foreign tourists within the Latin America region, and ranks eighth in the world. It captured 15.7% of the Americas' international tourism market, second only to the U.S. The vast majority of Mexico's tourists come from the United States and Canada.

Back in 1900, an American colony formed along the shores of Lake Chapala, about an hour from Guadalajara. Retirees seeking a reprieve from icy North American climes discovered they could live both better and cheaper in Mexico. And by clustering together, they had a sense of security and they didn't even have to speak Spanish.

The word got out that life was good south of the border and American compounds sprung up throughout Mexico. Cuernavaca, the "Eternal Spring" haven for the wealthy from Mexico City, also caught on with rich Americans and other foreigners. Then came the classy colonial cities of Guanajuato, San Miguel de Allende, Querétaro, Morelia and Aguascalientes with their double draws of great weather and outstanding cultural attractions.

Guanajuato, built by silver barons, is prized for its narrow cobblestone streets and historic mansions. The University of Guanajuato, with its arts programs and 15,000 students, also adds a touch of class to the expatriates' second hometown.

San Miguel de Allende, however, is the epitome of an American colony in Mexico. More than 5,000 mostly well-to-do Americans, about 10% of the population, call Mexico's "national monument" home at least for half of the year. They were drawn by the famed artists' colony, the perfect climate and clear air, the picturesque village with its classic colonial structures as well as the verdant hills that envelop the community.

And they don't have to speak Spanish, even though many had come to learn the idiom at a variety of language schools. There's an English newspaper, one of the largest bilingual libraries in the country, cable TV with American programming, golf courses and tennis courts and, within an hour's drive, there's even a Wal-Mart and a Costco.

There's no place in Mexico that's free of gringo influence. The most remote villages can claim American residents. However, most Americans settle in comfort zones where they can live with others from the States.

The growing gringo market has attracted real estate companies from the U.S., developers and promoters, and a whole assortment of salesmen on the Internet. They put out claims that Mexico is like the U.S. -- 50 years ago.

There are brochures and magazines that claim: "You can retire in style and live better than you do now for as little as $694 a month. You can have a maid, a gardener, a driver – all on a Social Security budget." They say it's not news to an estimated 500,000 American retirees who now have their Social Security checks sent to them. They cite property taxes of $300, and car insurance of $540 a year and all-inclusive health care that costs $270. And that a full gourmet dinner won't cost more than $20.

They insist that the bad news perpetuated by television, the images of corruption, checkpoints with guns and officials swayed by bribery, doesn't give a true picture of modern Mexico.

Mexico's beaches always have been a drawing card for tourists. Acapulco was a buzz word for America's rich and famous for nearly a century. But much of Mexico's vast shoreline went largely undeveloped until the 1970s.

Then came Fonatur (Fondo Nacional de Fomento al Turismo) with a plan to convert a fisherman's island surrounded by dense jungle into a tourist center. Cancun was born in 1974, and its continued success has resounded throughout the coastal areas.

Today there are gringo colonies of 5,000 or more in at least a dozen coastal cities, from the Mexican Riviera to the southern tip of Baja California. Million dollar mansions have sprung up along the dramatic cliffs overlooking the Pacific Ocean.

Fonatur's planned approach, which gave priority to the construction of major commercial airports, opened up Mexico's coasts to large-scale development. Five-star hotels and condo complexes, along with large swaths of groomed signature golf courses, have pushed aside the cactus and scrubland of the coastal deserts.

A whole generation of American tourists now equates the Mexican experience with Cancun, Puerto Vallarta, Ixtapa, Huatulco or Los Cabos. They take direct flights from scores of U.S. hubs, and in a couple of hours they're out of the snow and onto the beach. They stay in all-inclusive resorts, with meals, drinks and entertainment included in the tab. They buy souvenirs at the front desk and they never have to stray into the quaint but impoverished villages where the Mexican workers live.

Since its founding three decades ago, Fonatur has made tourism one of the most dynamic sectors of the Mexican economy, creating thousands of jobs, generating foreign revenue and impacting regional development.

The major resort destinations now account for 40% of the country's five-star hotels and generate 54% of the total revenue from foreign tourists.

Fonatur put up more than $1 billion for infrastructure projects. The agency built airports, roads and sewer and water lines and it backed loans of another $1.2 billion to construct hotels and condos, restaurants and golf courses at the five major resorts by the mid-1990s. That seed money soon generated $2.5 billion in outside investments.

It also created jobs for at least 150,000 Mexicans. Fonatur's intent was to mine Mexico's principal natural resources – its sun and seashores – and it figured that foreign investment and millions of tourists would flow to the vacation destinations. But there still was another benefit from the projects. They would help stem the tide of mass migration to Mexico's metropolitan areas.

Fonatur's first mega project has proven to be a huge success. Cancun, before 1970, was no more than a deserted sand-spit shaped like a lucky "7".

There was a fishing village nearby called Puerto Juárez that consisted of a couple of dozen shacks.

Fonatur put up $450 million in infrastructures and within two decades it got a return of $3 billion on its investment along with drawing 1.5 million tourists a year.

Today Cancun is a community of 500,000 residents who host more than 4 million visitors a year. It now generates 30% of the country's tourism revenue.

On a typical day, 190 flights, many of them direct charter or commercial jets from the United States, land at the Cancun airport, packed with tourists seeking a week, or maybe just a weekend, of fun in the sun and surf in a foreign country.

Well, it's not so foreign. There are McDonalds and Starbucks and Wal-Marts and Costcos and scores of familiar high-rise hotel franchises – with more than 20,000 rooms – as well as condos and restaurants where everyone speaks English.

Fonatur went on to develop five other vacation destinations along the Pacific Coast – Puerto Vallarta, Ixtapa, Los Cabos, Loreto and Huatulco. All are resorts of distinction, and together are worth billions and attract millions of tourists each year. But while none can match Cancun's impact, each has its own drawing card.

Cabo San Lucas, at the tip of the Baja California peninsula, was a fly-in fisherman's haven, the home of record-setting black and blue marlins. But back in the 1970s there was no paved road and the surrounding land was mostly barren desert that rippled down to abandoned beaches.

A billion dollars in investments changed all that, and by the 1990s the permanent population had gone from 6,000 to 50,000, some 30 major resorts boasted 3,200 rooms and counted 315,000 visitors by 1996. Four-lane highways replaced the dirt roads, the 20-mile stretch between Cabo San Lucas and San José bustled with condo construction, new golf courses transformed patches of desert sand to green, and a marina with moorings for 500 vessels commanded the center of the city.

Deep-sea anglers from all over the world are still drawn to the fertile waters off Land's End where some 40,000 marlin, some in the 400-pound class, are caught – and released -- each year. However, these days golfers and sunbathers vastly outnumber fishermen.

Huatulco was a real find for the Fonatur folks. They scouted the Oaxaca coastline by airplane and were amazed at the undiscovered vista below. Between two rivers which cascaded down the mountains were nine protected bays, and more than three dozen coves and beaches with untracked sand that stretched for miles.

Mexico's new Cancun was about to be born.

Except, they pledged, it would never resemble Cancun. Two-thirds of the land, including the waterfront, would remain untamed. Of the 52,000 acres, about 40,000 will be set aside to maintain ecological balance. There will be no high-rise hotels. The tallest building will be four stories. There have been construction delays, but the Fonatur master plan, if all goes well, forecasts completion of the project sometime after 2018, and it envisions Huatulco becoming Mexico's top vacation draw, bigger even than Cancun.

Fonatur planners admit that Cancun, for all its success, has its flaws. Chief among them is the concentration of development. They say they've learned their lesson. Nature, they say, will remain Huatulco's most important resource.

Fonatur now is embarking on an even more dramatic systematic planned development, this time both on and off shore. Its focus is on the Mar de Cortés, or the Gulf of California, that Jacques Cousteau called "The aquarium of the world."

The nautical tourism corridor, stretching more than 800 miles, is being labeled the largest sustainable regional tourist project yet. More than a score of ports, on both sides of the Gulf, from San Blas in southern Nayarit to San Felipe in the northern Baja, will be involved in marina and land developments.

When it gets underway, it promises to draw thousands of up-scale tourists who at least will have sea legs, if not their own yachts, to watch the whales and fish for marlin.

And it's assumed that most of these eco-tourists, like the millions of visitors who went before them, will be North Americans.

---

## Chapter One: TOURISM: Among the sources cited:

International Living, Waterford, Ireland, "Why one million Americans are moving to Mexico," 2008.

Fondo Nacional de Fomento al Turismo, Mexico, D.F., "Huatulco," "Cancun," March 28, 2008.

CNN Money.com, "San Miguel de Allende, Mexico," May 5, 2003.

Travelers Guide to Mexico, Mexico Government Tourism Office, 2006.

Lonely Planet, Berkeley, CA, "Mexico: a travel survival kit," 1992.

National Geographic, "Emerging Mexico: A special Issue," August 1996.

A poster calling for an end to violence against women in Ciudad Juárez stands in front of the Mexican consulate in El Paso, Texas. More than 800 females, between the ages of 12 and 22, most of them maquiladora workers, were murdered in the 1990s, and few of the killings have ever been solved.

# Chapter Two

## *The Drug Wars – 1*

♦

### *Innocents caught in drug wars' crossfire*

Rosa still has recurring nightmares from her years in Ciudad Juárez.

She's now living in Colorado, just outside of Denver, with her three young children. They're in school and doing well, on most days. She's not. She's constantly reminded of the violence she left behind in 2008. The evening television news and the newspaper headlines blurt out the horrors occurring on a daily basis in Juárez, just across the Rio Grande from El Paso, Texas.

El Paso, with a population of 600,000, has been considered one of the safest cities of its size. It recorded only 15 murders in 2008. Juárez, with a burgeoning population of 1.5 million, is a slaughterhouse. There were more than 1,300 murders, most of them gruesome public slayings, in 2008. That's 25 drug-related deaths each week.

Rosa's husband, Eduardo, was one of those victims. He had gone downtown to shop for a first communion dress for their seven-year-old daughter, and as he crossed the plaza just behind a police car, a violent explosion ripped apart the vehicle, sending shards of shrapnel in every direction. The patrol car was the target of a rocket-propelled grenade in broad daylight in the city square.

Eduardo was hit in the neck and face and died in a pool of blood.

Rosa remembers feeling numb as she watched an armored military truck pull up to their two-room, concrete block house on the edge of an industrial park. A soldier with a bullet-proof vest and carrying an automatic weapon walked cautiously up to the door. He told Rosa that her husband had died, and that four policemen had been murdered and that the killers reportedly were cops on the same force.

The drug war had come home with a vengeance.

Juárez was and still is the epicenter of drug cartel violence. Three major cartels, Sinaloa, Gulf and Juarez, are viciously vying for control of the most lucrative corridor for cocaine, marijuana and other drugs to the U.S. market.

It was no secret that lots of cops had been corrupted by cartel cash. A policeman's pay was but a pittance compared to that of drug cartel enforcers.

Rosa also was well aware of the increased violence and killings throughout Juárez. But her husband wasn't involved in drugs. He worked in a *maquiladora*. He was a family man. The cartels murdered their rivals, along with selected authority figures, like cops and judges, politicians and journalists.

Eduardo was an innocent victim. But he was just as dead.

Rosa's thoughts raced back to when they first met. They were teenagers, living on adjoining ranches on the outskirts of Chihuahua. Both came from big families. Eduardo was the youngest of 12 children and Rosa was the middle child of nine. Chihuahua was one of the most prosperous cities in Mexico, drawing its wealth from cattle, timber and mining.

But there wasn't enough wealth on their families' ranches to go around by the time they finished high school. So they got married and set off for the big city to the north. Ciudad Juárez, just across the Rio Bravo from the United States, was promoting employment opportunities in its assembly industries.

The *maquiladoras* were big business, and Juárez at the time had the largest "twin plant" labor force on the frontier, with about 250,000 workers in more than 300 plants, mostly owned and operated by major U.S. companies.

The twin cities of Juárez and El Paso long have had close ties, deeply interwoven by culture, trade and geography. Spanish is the first language for the majority on both sides of the Rio Grande. Many residents claim to hold dual citizenship and have relatives in both countries.

Just a few years ago, as many as 200,000 people a day crossed the river along one of the five bridges connected the two cities. Mexican nationals spent about $2.2 billion per year in El Paso, and before the bloodbath began, Americans fueled a vibrant tourism economy in Juárez. The drug wars changed all that.

The population of Juárez had soared, doubling in a decade to more than a million people. Municipal services couldn't keep up with the growth, and vast slums without electricity, running water or sanitary sewers sprouted along rutted paths. At one time it was estimated that 40% of the newcomers were squatters.

Both Rosa and Eduardo readily found work in separate assembly plants, conveniently located in the same industrial park, and while their wages were nowhere near what their company colleagues earned in the U.S., by working long hours, they were able to afford to rent a decent apartment.

But then Rosa became pregnant, had complications and couldn't return to her job. With only one salary, they couldn't pay the rent, and they were forced to move out of the apartment into a two-room shack near his workplace. Then a second child was born, and two years later, a third. All girls.

It was a dangerous neighborhood. No place to bring up girls, they agreed. But they had little choice.

Rosa had made a number of friends while she was at work on the assembly line. She befriended one young woman from Chihuahua named Margarita whose husband had gone north to Minnesota to find work, after his *maquiladora* plant was shuttered and the jobs were sent to China.

Margarita babysat Rosa's girls twice a week when her assembly shifts permitted. Margarita usually worked at night, and while she had to walk several miles to her house down darkened, muddy paths, she said she was rarely afraid.

But she didn't show up one Sunday morning at Rosa's place for coffee. Police found her body in a ditch later that day. She had been raped and strangled.

It wasn't a rare occurrence. Violence, especially against women, had been on the increase in Juárez since 1993. Within a decade, more than 800 females, between the ages of 12 and 22, turned up dead or missing. Most of them worked in the *maquiladoras* and most of the murders have gone unsolved.

Rosa begged her husband to quit his job and move away from Ciudad Juárez. Eduardo said someday they would go to the United States. He knew of several co-workers who had made it to Colorado and had landed high-paying jobs.

But he wasn't that anxious to go quite yet. He also knew of one friend who didn't make it out of the desert. He thought of him often, especially on the Day of the Dead. That's when there was a special mass right on the border.

The date was Nov. 2, 2003, *"El Dia de los Muertos,"* and the five Catholic bishops of Juárez, El Paso, San Antonio, Laredo and Las Cruces were con-celebrating a memorial mass for those migrants who died trying to reach the U.S.

Simple wooden eucharistic tables, altars nearly touching but divided by a 12-foot-high chain link fence, were set up on the sandy border at nearby Anapra, New Mexico. U.S. Border Patrol helicopters hovered overhead, raising plumes of dust and drowning out the prayers of the faithful. Teens on the Mexican side climbed and clung onto the  fence, teasing the American authorities who were monitoring the gathering.

Rosa and Eduardo joined several hundred people in the desert in prayer that day to end the border barrier. Mexicans and Americans, in equal numbers on both sides, grasped fingers through the chain link fence to recite the Our Father in English and Spanish.

Then they raised white wooden crosses with the names of the migrants – more than 400 – whose bodies had been discovered in the desert that year.

More than 2,800 people had died along the 2,000-mile frontier in the previous decade trying to get to the United States to get a job to keep their children from starving. Bishop Armando Ochoa of El Paso noted that the dead were only poor people trying to achieve human dignity.

Eduardo's eyes flooded with tears as he held his cross up high. He knew his friend, Guillermo Mendez, was there in spirit.

But Eduardo just wasn't ready to risk his life. And he sure didn't want to put his wife and three young daughters in danger.

Besides, he had gotten a promotion at work and things were looking up. If he made foreman, his family could move out of that slum dwelling and into a better neighborhood.

While Ciudad Juárez was rapidly turning into a most dangerous place, there still were parts of the city that were quite safe. The population had soared to more than 1,500,000, and although the vast majority of the new residents were dirt poor, Juárez did have pockets of wealth. Eduardo realized he'd never be able to afford a place in a gated community, nor would the girls be able to attend private schools. But, if they took care, they could have a decent life, as least by Mexican standards.

He bought a car. It was an old Toyota with a cracked windshield and a caved-in trunk, but it only cost about 1,000 pesos. He could take his family on a Sunday picnic in the countryside and have a brief respite from the squalor of the city.

Juárez had become a major conduit for the illegal drug trade and corruption was endemic among the police force, city officials and even the judiciary. The stage was being set for an organized crime takeover. The three major cartels of narcotraffickers – Sinaloa, Gulf and Juárez – had moved in for the showdown over who would command the prized "plaza," the drug smuggling lane to the U.S., the world's largest narcotics market.

Rosa and Eduardo kept their distance from the fray. They mostly stayed indoors and kept a close watch on their daughters. But they couldn't avoid the news, or the rumors, and each day the violence seemed to escalate.

They were most disturbed when they heard about armed men storming a Red Cross operating room in Juárez. They ordered the doctors and nurses performing surgery on a 25-year-old gunshot victim to leave, and then they killed the man.

Rosa again pleaded with her husband to get out of Juárez. They could go back to Chihuahua, to the peaceful countryside where their families still lived. But she said she was willing to go anyplace, even if they had to cross the Rio Bravo into the United States illegally.

She became even more adamant about leaving when she was told about four elementary schools being temporarily closed due to threats from gangs that were taking advantage of the widespread fear of the cartels. The thugs had demanded that teachers hand over their year-end bonuses – or their students would be kidnapped.

Their oldest daughter, Alicia, was in kindergarten at Elena Garro, one of the schools targeted. Rosa insisted she never return to that class.

Eduardo agreed. He finally was ready to go. He had been talking at work about a former colleague who had recently moved to Colorado, had landed a good job in construction and was making $12 an hour. Eduardo didn't make that much money in two days at the *maquiladora*.

Several guys at work told him how to get across the border, how to secure forged identification, how to contact a "coyote" to guide him and his family through the U.S. Border Patrol.

Eduardo told Rosa they would leave for the U.S. in two weeks, right after Alicia received her first communion at the parish church. Their daughter was excited about the event. She was going to walk down the aisle in a store-bought white dress, with a white lace veil covering her head and white sandals on her feet.

Eduardo said he was going downtown to shop for that outfit for his Alicia. He never made it into the store.

Rosa wept as she walked down the church aisle with her daughter. The next day she led the three girls across the Rio Bravo bridge into El Paso. She told them to never look back.

Three days later they arrived at the house of her husband's friend in Denver, Colorado.

# Chapter Two

## *The Drug Wars -2*

✦

### *Partners in crime claim 6,290 victims*

Mexicans and Americans are partners in crime.

Ninety per cent of the cocaine abused in the United States comes from Mexico. Ninety per cent of the weapons used to kill cops and rivals in Mexico to keep the drugs flowing north comes from the U.S.

It's a terrible partnership.

In 2008, some 6,290 people were murdered in the *narco*-related violence in Mexico. That's the official count. It's double that of the previous year. Within two months into 2009, the death toll already exceeded one thousand.

U.S. officials admit that 90% of the firearms recovered from the crime scenes in Mexico originated in the U.S.

There are huge billboards at most U.S. border checkpoints that warn motorists that possession of a firearm in Mexico could mean a prison sentence. Yet, the Bureau of Alcohol, Tobacco, Firearms and Explosives has traced more than 62,000 firearms seized in Mexico to U.S. sources.

In November of 2008 the Mexican army made the largest seizure of drug-cartel weapons in history from a house in Reynosa, just across the U.S. border from McAllen, Texas.. The cache included 540 rifles, 165 grenades, 500,000 rounds of ammunition and 14 sticks of dynamite. The weapons reportedly belonged to the Gulf cartel.

There were reports that the drug cartel thugs were better armed than the Mexican police or military. They were a lot better paid, too.

Forbe's 2009 list of the richest people in the world includes a fugitive don from Mexico who goes by the name of "Shorty." Joaquín Guzmán Loera, 54, head of the feared Sinaloa cartel, escaped from a Mexican prison back in 2001, days before he was to be extradited to the U.S.

The U.S. government offered a $5 million reward for his capture. That's pocket change for Guzmán whose net worth was estimated at $1 billion. Forbes listed his industry as "shipping."

The drug trade is big business.

It's estimated that the illegal drugs that flow across the Mexican border to the world's largest narcotics market are worth in excess of $23 billion. The Mexican connection supplies 90% of the cocaine, 80% of the methamphetamine and half of the marijuana used in the U.S., according to the Drug Enforcement Administration

The U.S. Government Accountability Office estimates that on the average 275 metric tons of cocaine arrives in Mexico for transshipment to the U.S. every year. Only about 36 metric tons are seized. Nineteen tons of "export quality" heroin is produced in Mexico but less than one ton is seized. Some 9,400 metric tons of marijuana is produced in Mexico each year, and only 2,700 tons are seized.

Behind the numbers and the surging violence is a shift in the way drugs are delivered to the United States. In the 1990s, the flow moved away from the Colombian distribution channels to networks in Mexico. Increased interdiction of the Colombian delivery routes and the opening of the U.S. border to trade put Mexico at the helm of the Western Hemisphere's lucrative drug trade.

And it wasn't long before organized crime moved in to compete – and kill – for the narco dollars. The lines were drawn when Mexico's most-wanted man, "Shorty" Guzmán, head of the Pacific-coast Sinaloa cartel, declared war on drug baron Vicente Carrillo Fuentes and sent his foot soldiers north to drive out the Juárez cartel. The Gulf cartel, based around the Gulf of Mexico coast, joined in on the fight.

The vicious drug wars erupted throughout the country in 2008, but especially along the northern frontier, the staging areas for narcotics distribution to the U.S. Ciudad Juárez was especially bloody, with its death toll reaching more than 1,300 that year.

While most of the dead were on the payroll or at least had connections with organized crime, hundreds of police, soldiers, government officials, judges and journalists have been assassinated when they challenged the cartels.

Widespread corruption in the ranks of law enforcement and throughout the political system stymied the efforts of federal government to reign in the murderous gangs. Cops have assassinated cops from the same department. Even judges and government officials have been discovered on the take from the cartels.

Juárez Mayor José Reyes, determined to counter the terror in his city, demanded that the city police department clean house. More than 400 cops were dismissed, and every officer had to undergo drug tests and background checks. He then requested federal troops in an attempt to restore order in the community. The army then took charge of Mexico's most violent city. The army in November of 2008 also was called in to disarm and lockdown the municipal police force in Matamoros, just across the border from Brownsville, Texas.

The cartels operate largely with impunity. Their hit men have gunned down their rivals, police officers and prosecutors, often in broad daylight. Reportedly only 2% of the murders in Mexico are ever solved.

Some slayings are most gruesome. In December 2008, a few days before Christmas, 12 decapitated bodies were found along a major boulevard in Chilpancingo, not far from Acapulco. It was only hours before the Guerrero governor was to participate in a religious procession in the area. Most of the dead were identified as soldiers from a nearby military base. Earlier, another 12 decapitated bodies were found outside of Mérida, Yucatan.

The assassins left a message on the scene: "For every one of mine that you kill, I will kill 10."

One day in February 2009, the cartels' hit men murdered 24 federal police, soldiers and governmental officials in an apparent coordinated attack in six major cities throughout Mexico. They used rocket-powered grenades, homemade bombs and automatic weapons.

The level of violence escalated shortly after Mexican President Felipe Calderón took office in late 2006. He declared war on the drug cartels and made the fight against crime his   No. 1 priority. He sent the army first to his home state of Michoacán, and then to Monterrey, Sinaloa and cities along the U.S. border. In early 2009 he bolstered the federal force with 45,000 soldiers dedicated to the war on drugs.

One Mexican official noted that if Calderón hadn't intensified the battle against the cartels, the next president of Mexico likely could be a narcotrafficker.

While the crackdown has spurred the cartels to escalate the violence in some areas, it now is seen as an act of desperation. There are signs that the government is gaining an upper hand.

"El Capo Caramuela," also known as Gregorio Sauceda Gamboa, a major figure in the Gulf cartel, was taken into custody in February 2009 in Reynosa. The cartel's boss, Osiel Cardenas Guillen, was extradited to the U.S. in 2007 along with 40 other narcotraffickers.

Jaime Gonzales, the founder of a gang of Gulf cartel hit men, army deserters called Zetas, also was arrested in Reynosa.

The Mexican Drug Enforcement Administration cut into the sources and profits of the cartels by seizing assets valued at nearly $500 million. The

DEA also seized 34 tons of cocaine in two separate operations. The net effect of the seizures contributed to a 44% price increase for cocaine in the U.S.

The increased military presence in Ciudad Juárez, more than 5,000 troops, cut the death rate from 10 to one or two murders a day.

The Mexican government spent $6.5 billion in the past two years to combat drug trafficking and has started to see some results, according to Eduardo Medina-Mora, Mexico's attorney general. The price of cocaine in the U.S. doubled while its purity dropped 35%. Mexico crippled the methamphetamine trade by banning certain chemicals.

He said the worst might soon be over as world's most powerful drug cartels melt down while engaging in turf wars and fighting off an unprecedented crackdown by the Mexican government.

Medina-Mora said the Mexican government didn't expect to stop drug trafficking, but it hoped to make it so difficult that smugglers no longer use Mexico as their conduit to the U.S. He said in February 2009 that the conflict had peaked, but the country wouldn't reach its objective until Mexican citizens feel they have achieved "tranquility."

There's at least one border city in the 2,000-mile frontier where the drug war ebbed in 2008. Nuevo Laredo, across the river from its Texas counterpart, experienced a dramatic drop in killings, from 180 in 2006 to just 55 in 2008.

It wasn't because of a governmental crackdown, or a military enforcement. Rather, it was the result of a cease-fire and a "business" accord between two cartels that were decimating their ranks by bloodily vying for that drug corridor to the U.S.

The Sinaloa cartel had been trying to muscle into Nuevo Laredo, which was controlled by the Gulf cartel. They wanted access to Laredo, the busiest trade port along the U.S.-Mexican border, where it's relatively easy to smuggle drugs inside some of the 6,000 commercial trucks that travel south-to-north each day.

For four years the violence escalated. The new police chief was murdered hours after he was sworn in. Thugs murdered the editor of the daily newspaper, and rival cartel gangs used rocket-propelled grenades in street battles.

Then suddenly in 2007 the turf war ended. The two cartels decided it wasn't good for business. They were spending too much time killing and too little conducting their criminal enterprises. So they agreed to share the spoils.

The Sinaloans agreed to pay a tax to the Gulf cartel to use the Laredo border crossing. They also agreed to move upriver to try to wrest control of Juárez from the Juárez cartel.

Nuevo Laredo's Mayor Ramon Garza was pragmatic. He was pleased that the violence in his city had subsided but he realized that the drug cartels have not gone away. Rather, it's now business as usual. The traffickers smuggle cocaine and marijuana across the river, mostly mind their own affairs, and Mexican authorities – some of whom are on the take – look the other way.

Tourism and investments in Nuevo Laredo are on the rebound. There's a new Wal-Mart and new cultural and civic centers, and the old train station has been transformed into a literature center. It was inaugurated in September of 2008 by Latin America's literary giant, Gabriel Garcia Marquez.

While Nuevo Laredo's good fortune now contributes to Ciudad Juárez's plague, U.S. counternarcotics agents anticipate that the combatants in Juárez, too, will tire of their bloodletting – sooner or later.

But meanwhile, the United States took steps to assure that Mexico's drug war stays below the border in early 2009.

Officials focused their eyes on that West Texas corridor, the key shipping and distribution center for drugs destined for markets throughout much of the U.S. Its strategic location had become a magnet for organized crime.

The Obama Administration bolstered its official presence in the area by sending 37 agents from the Bureau of Alcohol, Tobacco and Firearms to the region along with the reassigning 90 officers of the Immigration and Customs Enforcement Agency (ICE) to the frontier.

Governors in the border states are concerned about a spillover of drug-related violence. There have been kidnappings in Phoenix and killings in Atlanta, and there was talk of sending the National Guard to further militarize the border area.

Mexico's drug wars have already breached the border. The U.S. Justice Department National Drug Intelligence Center reported that six cartels, 129 midlevel organizations and 606 local groups were engaged in drug trafficking activities in 2008.

Authorities say that there are 195 U.S. cities in Mexican drug-trafficking network, with Atlanta as the new gateway to the troubled Southwest border. That city's network of stash houses make it the principal narcotics distribution center for the entire eastern U.S.

U.S. officials are hoping that the first installment in a $1.4 billion package, signed into law as the Mérida Initiative in June 2008, will pay dividends in combating international drug trafficking and related violence, both in Mexico and in the U.S. The first stage in a multi-year program provides $400 million to Mexico, as well as $65 million to Central America and the Caribbean.

The money will pay for helicopters and surveillance aircraft to support interdiction and rapid response of Mexican law enforcement agencies. It also will be used for non-intrusive inspection equipment, ion scanners and canine units for Mexican customs along with funds for a new Mexican federal police and military unit to interdict trafficked drugs, arms, cash and persons.

The real source of Mexico's drug-induced migraine, of course, is the marketplace, and the insatiable appetite of Americans for illegal narcotics. One study reported that 35 million Americans aged 12 and older had tried cocaine at least once. However, that same study said that overall illicit drug use among teens was down 23% since 2001.

The U.S. 2008 budget for drug control amounts to about $13 billion, and the focus and funds are split between reducing demand through treatment and prevention, bolstering domestic law enforcement and for interdiction at the border and at home.

As for those thousands of illegal weapons which were smuggled into Mexico from U.S. sources and which resulted in a bloodbath for thousands, the United States was working with the Mexican government on a $1.2 million plan to develop an explosives and firearms detection canine facility as well as enhanced training to detect firearms shipments inside Mexico.

Also in the works was the widespread implementation of "eTrace," a firearms tracing system which is able to identify purchasers, traffickers, networks and patterns so law enforcement can target and dismantle the infrastructure supplying firearms to the drug cartels in Mexico.

---

## Chapter Two: THE DRUG WARS: Among the sources cited:

Associated Press, Acapulco, Mexico, "12 decapitated bodies found in southern Mexico," Dec. 22, 2008.

Arian Campo-Flores, Newsweek, "Bloodshed on the border," Dec. 8, 2008

Ioan Grillo, Time, "Stitching up bullet wounds in Mexico's drug war," Dec. 29, 2008

John Burnett, National Public Radio, "Nuevo Laredo returns to normal as violence slows," Jan. 23, 2009

Agencia El Universal, The Brownsville (Tx) Herald, "Mexican army disarms Matamoros police," Nov. 13, 2008

U.S. Embassy Mexico City Reports, "Combating illicit firearms," September 2008

Larry Copeland, USA Today, "Mexican cartels plague Atlanta," Feb. 27, 2009

David Montero, Christian Science Monitor, "Journalists targeted in latest Mexico drug violence," Oct. 13, 2008

Texas residents, farmers and ranchers along Hwy. 281 in the Rio Grande Valley were overwhelmingly opposed to the U.S. building a border wall on the edge of their property.

# Chapter Three

## *The Border -1*

✦

### *Once much of the U.S. was part of Mexico*

Rosita Morelos is fond of saying that she didn't cross the border. The border crossed her.

Her great-great grandfather lived in San Antonio. It was called Mision San Antonio de Valero back then, and it was part of Mexico. There were lots of Mexicans living in Texas long before the Alamo.

Even the Alamo belonged to Mexico. Those American textbook heroes including James Bowie and Davy Crockett were actually trespassers. Few really remember the Alamo as it was: a Mexican mission that was turned into a Mexican military compound.

Nor do they readily recall the map of Mexico of 1835. The country was a whole lot bigger, like 40% larger than today.

Stephen Austin started it all in 1821 when he recruited 300 German immigrant families to settle in vast plains of southern Texas. The colony became the foundation of Anglo-American presence in Texas and within the next 14 years, U.S. settlers came to outnumber Mexicans by a four to one margin.

The new colonists bristled under Mexican rule and established a provisional government with Sam Houston at the helm. Political struggles evolved into armed rebellion. Gen. Martin Perfecto de Cos was sent to subdue the rebellious "Texians" but his troops couldn't accomplish it.

That so angered Mexico's president, dictator and Gen. Antonio Lopez de Santa Ana that he decided to lead a force of 4,000 troops to oust the band of rag-tag rebels who had taken over the Alamo. The Alamo "defenders," all 189 of them, were killed. They didn't stand a chance.

However, 46 days later Gen. Houston and his army, remembering the Alamo, wiped out Santa Ana's forces at the Battle of San Jacinto in just 18 minutes of fighting. Santa Ana, in exchange for his freedom, agreed to grant Texan independence.

The Republic of Texas was annexed to the United States in 1845, becoming the 28th state. Its borders were redrawn to include what is now New Mexico and California. When Mexico resisted that expansionist policy, American troops landed at Veracruz, and just as Spanish conquistador Hernán Cortés had done three centuries earlier, they moved on to Mexico City, staging their final victorious battle in 1847 at Chapultepec Castle.

The following year the Treaty of Guadalupe Hidalgo was signed, requiring Mexico to cede its territories north of the Rio Grande. It was an enormous area, encompassing the present-day states of Arizona, New Mexico, California, Nevada, Utah and part of Colorado.

Five years later, Santa Ana set out to raise much needed capital for his country, crippled by war and a weakened economy, by ceding more land to the United States, for a price. He negotiated the Gadsen Purchase in 1853 which delivered the Mesilla Valley, today's Arizona and southern New Mexico, to the U.S. for $10 million.

It marked his final undoing. Santa Ana, Mexican president off and on for the previous 22 years, was ousted from power in 1855.

Thus, over the course of two decades, the United States had acquired more than 500,000 square miles of Mexican land, a territory equivalent in size to Western Europe. At the same time, the U.S. had absorbed 100,000 Mexican citizens and 200,000 Native Americans living there.

Rosita Morales' great-great grandfather was one of those Mexicans who became an American through conquest. She remembers her mother relating his adventures living in San Antonio – with all those Germans. It wasn't long before he moved south of the border. He settled in Matamoros, just across the Rio Bravo from Brownsville, Texas.

He was more comfortable on the Mexican side. There were too many foreigners living in Texas. Immigrants from Europe had changed the complexion of San Antonio. Street signs were in English, German and Spanish and there were sections of town dominated by German architecture.

The Morales family, however, like other Tex-Mex Hispanics, could claim heritage on both sides of the border. Rosita's great-grandfather owned a cattle ranch on the Chisholm Trail near San Antonio and her grandfather, for awhile, ran a farm in Texas' fertile Rio Grande Valley.

Her own family pledged allegiance to two nations. Her parents were Mexicans, who lived in Matamoros for most of their lives. But they lived and worked in Texas for a number of years, and two of their children were born in the United States. That meant Rosita's big brother, Miguel Angel, and her little sister, María Guadalupe, were U.S. citizens. They grew up and went to school in Matamoros, Tamaulipas, but their birth certificates said they were Americans.

Rosita was born in Matamoros. Her birth certificate said she was Mexican. It didn't much matter, however, in those early years when the family seemed to straddle the border, moving wherever there was work.

She jokingly called her brother a "gringo." He was light skinned. She wasn't. Her sister was dark-skinned too, but María at an early age decided that she was an American, and she became determined to learn English. She was an "A" student in class, spent countless hours watching American movies, and regularly went downtown to practice her English with the tourists.

But as they grew up, Rosita and her siblings became well aware of their accidents of birth as they crossed the Rio Bravo into Brownsville to go shopping or to stop for a hamburger, French fries and a shake at McDonald's.

Miguel and María carried U.S. passports. Rosita stood in a longer line with her Mexican passport. Rosita acquired a U.S. border pass that allowed her to more easily cross into Brownsville. But the pass restricted her from traveling more than 25 miles north of the border, the site of U.S. immigration checkpoints.

Her siblings didn't have any such restrictions. They traveled unfettered between the two countries, once taking a bus to Corpus Christi to visit relatives. Rosita had to stay home.

Their situation was not all that uncommon for Hispanics along the frontier. Sisters and brothers and uncles and aunts live on both sides the border. Some are Americans; some are Mexicans. All speak Spanish; most speak English, as well. They attend school. They work. They shop. They visit friends and eat out. They take in a movie or a sports event or a concert.

On either side of the river.

The same people live in the Tex-Mex sister cities. They have relatives in Brownsville and in Matamoros; in McAllen and in Reynosa; in Laredo and in Nuevo Laredo; in El Paso and in Ciudad Juárez, as well as a score of other twin communities along the 2,000-mile U.S.-Mexico corridor.

For more than a century, the people of the border mixed freely. A river divided them in Texas but there were numerous bridges and crossings, and besides some parts of the Rio Grande were only a stone's throw across. There were fences, of course, but sometimes just a single strand of wire delineated the two countries. Sometimes it was difficult to tell the nations apart.

For years, Mexicali and Calexico in California were like one city, with a flimsy, chain-link fence between them. People would casually pull aside the fence and walk across the border. The 90-mile boundary between the fertile fields of the Imperial and Mexicali valleys at one time had a total of only six miles of fences.

Those twin communities – well, Mexicali is 20 times bigger – are one people. Some 60,000 of its residents carry border-crossing cards to shop in Calexico. About 80% of Calexico children enter school speaking Spanish. Half of the workforce in the Imperial Valley today comes from Mexico.

It's a similar story 1,500 miles or so to the east. The Rio Grande Valley is Hispanic on both sides of the river. The census claims 97% of the population of Starr County in Texas speaks Spanish.

The "twin" cities of Brownsville and Matamoros have long fostered a lot of cross-traffic. More than 85,000 Mexicans hold U.S. border permits, which allows them easy access to schools, work, shopping and dining in Brownsville and its environs. The U.S. consul in Matamoros estimates that 100,000 Americans -- "Winter Texans," spring breakers, business executives and tourists -- cross the bridges into Mexico each year.

Brownsville has a Mexican feel. Spanish is not the official language. It's just the everyday language. Billboards rarely sell products in English.

Rosita Morales didn't know a word of English until she started high school in Matamoros. Her English teacher didn't know much, either. It was a second language for everyone in the Valley.

Her parents lived and worked on both sides of the river. Her father labored in the sugar cane fields off U.S. Hwy. 83 and helped harvest the Rio Grande Valley's famed ruby red grapefruit groves near McAllen, Texas. But they preferred to live in Mexico.

Her brother Miguel Angel worked in an auto salvage yard, one of dozens which sprawl behind chain link fences, straddling U.S. Hwy. 83 near Progreso, a half-hour's drive from Brownsville. The "NAFTA Bridge" is nearby, and rusty transport carriers each day line up on the palm-studded boulevard to deliver their cargo of not-so-gently used cars and trucks with odometers rolled back, to central Mexico and beyond. Most make it to Guatemala where a select $200 clunker in the U.S. could command as much as $2,000.

Miguel Angel was single. He had a nice car, made a decent living by Valley standards and lived in a small apartment with his blonde girlfriend in McAllen.

Maria Guadalupe was in her early 20s when she left Matamoros. She was restless, and adventurous. She was at the top of her high school class and once had visions of going to college, that is until reality and money stood in the way. She got a job in a small pharmacy down the street from the border but never made more than $10 a day.

She had a cousin in Milwaukee, Wis., who worked for Harley Davidson Corp. and bragged about making more than $100 a day. So Maria took her

U.S. passport, said her goodbyes to her parents and her sister, Rosita, and got on a bus headed for Wisconsin.

Rosita was 25, and pregnant at the time with her second child. Her husband worked in a garage, off and on. He had a drinking problem, and often when he returned late at night to their one-room shack on the outskirts of Matamoros, he would become abusive. Rosita would confide in her little sister over the phone about her problems, and María often responded that she should leave her husband and come to live with her in Milwaukee.

But Rosita had two young children, and she felt close to her parents. Besides, she was a Mexican. Her sister was an American. Rosita's U.S. border pass would only take her a half-hour north of Brownsville before she'd be stopped by U.S. immigration officials.

Then one night her husband didn't come home. Two days went by, and then a week, and there was no word of his whereabouts. It was rumored that he had gotten involved with a drug cartel. The police were no help. The narcotics trade had fostered violence and widespread corruption in what once was placid border town. There were "missing" people everywhere.

Rosita waited another week before calling her sister in Milwaukee. Her husband didn't make much money, and sometimes his paycheck was cashed at a cantina, but at least most of the time there was something left over to feed the kids.

She was desperate. She didn't want to rely on her parents for help. They were poor, too. She called María Guadalupe. Her sister was working days, had gotten a raise, bought a car and was about to move into a bigger apartment. And yes, she said, there'd be plenty of room for her big sister and her two darling nieces.

Maria offered to drive to Brownsville to pick up Rosita and the kids and steer them around the immigration checkpoints and back to Wisconsin. The plan went without a hitch.

It was mid-January in 2004 when Rosita saw snow for the first time. It wasn't to be the last time that year. She landed a night job cleaning offices in downtown Milwaukee, and was paid $8 an hour. It was more than her husband made in a day.

She never saw that man again. She didn't see her folks, either. They couldn't get a visa to visit the United States. Rosita didn't have a visa either. María traveled back and forth to Mexico by plane each Christmas. Her sister stayed behind in Milwaukee with the two girls.

The three of them were "illegal aliens." Aunt María wasn't.

# Chapter Three

## *The Border -2*

✦

## *Great Wall, virtual fence corral migrants*

It's a long, long frontier. It stretches from sea to shining sea, from the Pacific to the Gulf, covering a total of 1,951 miles of mountains and plains, harsh deserts and rich, bountiful fields, passing in between tiny hamlets and burgeoning metropolises.

In Texas, the border, which measures more than 800 miles from Brownsville to El Paso, is defined by a hard-working river that sustains crops and people on both sides. The Americans call it Rio Grande; the Mexicans call it Rio Bravo.

The two nations may be different, but the people are the same. More than 90% of the frontier people are Latinos who speak Spanish a whole lot better than English. Most have kinfolk on both sides of the great divide. For most of their lives, they had easy access across the boundary line to work, shop and visit with friends and relatives.

No longer. A tall wall now separates them.

Seven hundred miles of barriers of concrete and steel have been strategically planted along the border. The initial cost in 2008 was $1.2 billion. But the total impact is still unknown. For the most part, the people of the frontier wanted no part of it. The people in Washington, D.C., ordered the wall instead of tackling long-overdue immigration reform.

It worked in California. Sort of. The "Tortilla Wall," as it's commonly called, thwarted the plans of thousands of would-be "illegal aliens." It's been in place ever since 1993, and by now probably several million immigrants have had to find another path into the United States. In 1992, some 202,000 undocumented immigrants were apprehended on the border; two years later, with that security fence in place, the numbers dropped to just 9,000.

The wall, a 10-foot fence of welded steel, starts out in the Pacific Ocean and runs 14 miles to the Otay Mesa Border Crossing. It was part of Operation Gatekeeper, which sealed much of the San Diego border back in 1993. A decade later it was deemed insufficient and a 14-foot secondary fence about 130 feet north of the existing barrier was constructed, although the stretch into the ocean was denied re-enforcement by the California Coastal Commission.

By 2005, a total of 80 miles of federally enforced barriers and fencing had been installed at strategic points on the border, mainly in Texas and California. But the "Tortilla Wall" was the longest.

Illegal immigration, of course, was not stopped in its tracks. In 2005 there were an estimated 11 million undocumented immigrants in the U.S., an increase of nearly four million since the 2000 census.

The escape routes just jogged around the barriers into the deserts and ever-dangerous environments where countless immigrants paid the price with their lives.

The "Tortilla Wall" gave a false sense of security. And, besides, as was later discovered, there were at least 40 tunnels under the great divide. Some tunnels under the fence were as deep as 80 feet and some more than a half-mile long They were busy thoroughfares for smuggling drugs and weapons, as well as immigrants.

One tunnel running from San Diego to Tijuana was highly sophisticated. It was eight feet tall, had a concrete floor, was wired for electricity and had drainage. It linked a modern warehouse on the California side with another in Tijuana. Tons of drugs were stored on both sides.

With the surge of millions of illegal aliens, the nation became embroiled in an acrimonious debate over how to resolve the immigration conundrum. One common element in both Republican and Democrat proposals, amplified by the war on terror, was border security.

Thus was the stage set for the Great Wall of Mexico.

The chairman of the House Armed Service Committee, Duncan Hunter, a California Republican, proposed building two parallel steel and wire fences running from the Gulf of Mexico to the Pacific Coast. It was to be a reinforced, two-layer 15-foot fence, separated by a 100-yard gap, running the entire length of the U.S. border with Mexico. The estimated price tag was $8 billion.

The final version in the Secure Fence Act of 2006, adopted by big margins in both the House and Senate and signed into law by President George W. Bush on Oct. 26, 2006, rolled back the additional fencing to 700 miles of the 2,000-mile border, and cut the price tag to $1.2 billion. The cost has since escalated to $1.6 billion, and will likely continue to rise.

A report from the Congressional Research Service stated that installing and maintaining the border wall and its surveillance technology could cost $49 billion over the next 25 years.

Nevertheless, it's a done deal. But it sure hasn't been overwhelmingly popular on either side of the border.

Then Mexican President Vincente Fox compared the barrier to the Berlin Wall and denounced it as "disgraceful and shameful." His Foreign Secretary Luis Ernesto Derbez said Mexico was not going to allow "a stupid thing like this wall."

Polls in the United States indicated that while border security was desirable in the wake of the 9-11 terrorist attack, a wall between neighbors was not the answer. Former New Mexico Gov. Janet Napolitano was fond of saying, "Show me a 15-foot fence and I'll show you a 16-foot ladder."

In general, the Americans who for years had lived and worked with the Mexicans on the frontier were against building the wall. Those living far from the border, including many who never visited it, were more inclined to support the barrier.

Texas Gov. Rick Perry opposed the idea, saying that instead of closing the border, new technology should be employed to support more legal and safe migration. The Laredo, Texas, city council unanimously opposed the wall expansion.

The Department of Homeland Security had to sue the border town of Eagle Pass, Texas, to allow construction of the fence alongside a city park. The city bills itself as the place where "Yeehaw! Meets Olé!" Its mayor has a sign in his office that says, "Don't Build Walls Between Amigos." Still, it's in line for a $10 million fence that splits the city park from the municipal golf course.

Over in Brownsville, where the University of Texas campus as well as Fort Brown, an historical battleground site of the Mexican-American war, were scheduled to be dissected by the wall, it would be hard to find any support for the scheme.

Plans called for a double fence, 16 feet high and 17 miles long, from the mouth of the Rio Grande north along the Brownsville-Matamoros border. It would also cut through the Fort Brown Golf Course, although there was a move to leave a gate open for easy access. It's a friendly place, and the golfers usually abide by the signs that advise them not to hit their balls over the Rio Grande and into Mexico.

University leaders were adamant in their opposition to the fence that could impact a $140 million expansion project. Besides, a large number of their students are from south of the border.

Faced with such widespread opposition, the Department of Homeland Security was forced to alter plans by shortening and rerouting the fence. The compromise assured the university of a 10-foot high barrier that incorporates technology security. The southern perimeter of the campus would be turned into a laboratory to test that technology.

Throughout the fertile fields and villages of the Rio Grande Valley, all along U.S. Hwy. 83, homemade signs simply stated "No Wall." But they got one, nevertheless. The feds convinced the ranchers and residents that the levees along the river needed to be bolstered for flood control. On the side facing Texas is a sloped 16-foot mound. Out of sight to Americans is the sheer 15-foot concrete and steel barrier that faces Mexico.

Many of the ranchers went to court to challenge the federal government's payment policy for taking some of the region's richest agricultural land to build the wall.

One section of the barrier was mistakenly constructed six feet inside Mexican territory, and had to be moved at a cost of $3 million.

The Rio Grande Valley, on both sides, is home to a wide variety of rare plant and animal species. It's on a major migratory path for birds and butterflies, and a stopover for Monarchs on their way to their winter haven in Central Mexico. The U.S. Fish and Wildlife Service reported that up to 75% of the protected lands and refuges in the Valley would be affected by the border wall.

Officials at the Santa Ana National Wildlife Refuge, a favorite spot for naturalists and birdwatchers, feared a fence would severely impact the movement of protected species across the frontier.

The Nature Conservancy, which owns 1,000 acres on the river, including the largest remaining forests of native sabal palm, also fought plans to erect an 18-foot tall, concrete and steel barrier through a mile of its preserve. The Conservancy's refuge is part of a 30-year plan to piece together public and private lands into a continuous wildlife corridor along the lower Rio Grande.

The Department of Homeland Security has softened its wall plans in some remote regions by opting for surveillance technology, access gates and more Border Patrol presence rather than constructing a wall where there's little border traffic.

In Arizona, a "virtual fence" with sensors, cameras and sophisticated communication networks, was planned along the entire border, with a completion date in 2012. It's a massive, costly project, with estimates running as high as $6.7 billion. The project got a bonus of $100 million from the economic stimulus package to speed up the process.

The high-tech "virtual fence" already has run into a number of snafus. A 28-mile test patch built in Arizona near Tucson had so many problems it had to be scrapped. Another trial was ordered along 30 miles in Ajo, Arizona.

The Great Wall and the "virtual fence" along with the homeland security they promise, are tied to the effectiveness of the U.S. Border Patrol, whose numbers have doubled to more than 18,000 in recent years. Recruiting and training has been accelerated to put more manpower on the frontier.

The current priority mission of the Border Patrol, which traces its beginnings to a handful of agents patrolling desolate areas on horseback in 1924, is to prevent terrorism. But the day-to-day mission is the apprehension of illegal immigrants. Since 1997, the Border Patrol has halted 12.8 million suspects.

In 2007, Border patrol agents arrested nearly 877,000 people illegally entering the United States. Agents also seized more than 14,241 pounds of cocaine and 1.8 million pounds of marijuana, with a combined street value of $1.6 billion.

The fences and heightened security at the border in 2008, along with a weaker U.S. economy, reduced the number of arrests – and likely attempts – of people trying to sneak into the United States. The Border Patrol caught 705,000, nearly 2,000 a day, the lowest number since 1976.

Border apprehensions peaked at 1.7 million in the mid-1980s, fell to about 1 million in the late 1980s, and hit 1.6 million again in 2000. Border Patrol staffing has climbed steadily to 18,000 agents from 4,000 in 1993.

The Great Wall of Mexico is not all wall. It's not a continuous structure, but rather a grouping of short physical walls that start and stop, secured in between by a system of stadium lights, sensors and cameras monitored by Border Patrol agents.

The wall traverses a variety of terrains, including urban areas and deserts, locations where the most concentrated numbers of illegal crossings and drug trafficking have been observed in the past. The urban focus has been on San Diego and El Paso, Texas.

Construction was on a fast track ever since the fall of 2006 when Congress authorized and funded the project. Several legislators attempted to stall the startup until a comprehensive border security plan was in place. Some favored slowing down the process until a new administration could be voted in, seated and heard. Assurances were given that the Department of Homeland Security would proceed "very cautiously." The DHS secretary said there would be an eight-month test of the "virtual fence" before any construction of a physical barrier.

There'd be no wall construction until late in the Bush presidency, if at all, he said.

But by late summer of 2008, some 344 miles of fencing had been completed. It consisted of 190 miles of pedestrian border fence and 154 miles of vehicle border barriers, mostly in New Mexico, Arizona and California.

The staunchest opposition to the wall emanated from the Rio Grande Valley in Texas, where rich agricultural land, in many cases handed down to family members for more than 200 years, runs to the banks of the Rio Grande.

By early December, earthen levees and concrete walls were going up along the river in Texas. Five hundred miles of fencing on the U.S. Southwest border had been completed.

President-elect Barack Obama said he wanted to evaluate the border project before giving the go-ahead for another 170 miles of fencing.

DHS Secretary Chertoff said there wouldn't be much left to do by the time Obama took office, adding that 600 miles would be completed by then.

---

## Chapter Three: THE BORDER: Among the sources cited:

Mimi Hall, USA Today, "Virtual fence gets second chance on U.S. border," March 11, 2009

U.S. Border Patrol Overview, Aug. 22, 2008

Jason Beaubein, National Public Radio, "Agents use high- and low-tech tracking at border," Jan. 28, 2009

Wikipedia, "Tortilla Wall," San Diego, CA, February 2008

John Burnett, National Public Radio, "Nature Conservancy fights planned border fence," Jan. 26, 2009

Christopher Sherman, Brownsville (TX) Herald, "Juries may decide prices," Nov. 13, 2008

Joseph Nevins, author, "Dying to Live: U.S. immigration in an age of global apartheid," 2008

Associated Press, Washington, D.C., "Southwest border fence reaches 500-mile mark," Dec. 17, 2008

Thomas Frank, USA Today, "Border detention the lowest since 1976," Dec. 29, 2008

Several bridges across the Rio Grande are under construction to accommodate direct truck traffic to and from the maquiladoras just inside the Mexican border. This old span links Brownsville and Matamoros on a narrow stretch of the river.

# Chapter Four

## *Maquiladoras -1*

✦

### *Made in America, south of the border*

Carlos Rodríguez looks forward to going to work every day in a plant in Reynosa, Tamaulipas. He likes his boss. He likes his colleagues. He likes his job. He likes the working conditions.

It's not the reaction most critics of *maquiladoras* have come to expect.

His is a new high-tech plant that makes stainless steel cabinetry for hospitals, universities and research labs. He was trained to operate a computer that guides lasers for precision designs and cuts.

Again, it's not your typical assembly plant.

Carlos makes about $1.50 an hour now. He got a 25-cent raise last year. He's heard all about the wages his company pays its workers back in Two Rivers, Wisconsin. It bothers him some, but he realizes it's not his business. Besides, most Mexicans don't earn as much as he does.

And the $1.50 an hour is more than he earned in a day back in his hometown, about eight hours to the southeast. Oh, some days he made a lot more as a boot-maker. But there were days when he made less. And he was the boss.

Carlos ran his leather goods shop out of the front room of his two-bedroom tiny house. His hired hands were his younger brother and two other teenage villagers. Often he couldn't pay them, but they got used to that. They had no other alternatives.

There were no industries in Tantoyuca, Veracruz. Once the village was the heart of a large, prosperous cattle ranch. But that was three generations ago. Carlos' great-grandfather owned lots of land and lots of cattle. He also had lots of children. Twelve survived. And they had lots of children, too. By the time Carlos came along, there were more than 100 descendants of great-grandpa Alejandro Rodriguez.

Now 200 acres and 200 cattle divided by 100 doesn't make anyone rich. Such is the story of Mexico then and now. A century ago, a ranch that size could support a family in luxury. Today, if all the children and grandchildren stayed in town, there'd just be too many mouths to feed.

Family is all-important to Mexicans. Most kids grow up and get married and have kids and never really leave the neighborhood. The cousins play with each other and visit grandma's house every day. Every other person in Tantoyuca  is named Rodriguez. They're all cousins. And even if the blood line is thin, they still call each other cousin.

Carlos is the second oldest of six children. His father is an alcoholic. His mother is a saint. His oldest sister, Maria, married young, had a couple of children and moved with her husband to Mexico City. He had a contact there who would give him a job in a nightclub. The pay was paltry. They lived in a shack in a teeming slum. The kids got sick and the neighborhood got violent, and one day Maria packed up the children and moved back to Tantoyuca. Her husband stayed behind in Mexico City. There were no jobs in the village.

Maria converted the living room of her modest concrete block house, with re-bars on the roof awaiting a third story, into a tiny storefront that sells candy and gum and pastries and pop. A bus stop on her doorstep draws some customers. On a good day she may make $2.

However, her kids are safe and healthy and happy. They don't see their father but one weekend a month, but their grandma is nearby, and so are dozens of their cousins.

There still are a couple of cattle ranches on the village outskirts, and there are a few jobs for cowboys on quarter horses at roundup time.  But, outside of the "penny capitalists" who sell eats and plastic trinkets from their homes and in open-air markets, most villagers have no visible means of support.

There is one cottage industry, however, that's popular if not productive with the Rodriguez clan. At least a dozen families are into boot making. Shoes, too. Purses, wallets, key chains, anything made with tooled leather produced by homegrown cattle. There's no factory in town. Everything is homemade.

Carlos still wears the hats of boss, cobbler and salesman even though now he's up on the Mexican border working 48 hours a week for an American company. On his Sundays off, he sits in a stall in the sprawling Reynosa market behind a sampling of boots and other leather products put together by his fledgling company in Tantoyuca. Sometimes he makes a sale. At the end of the day he gathers the goods and packs them away in the trunk of his car, a fenderless 1972 Ford with a shattered windshield.

He hopes that his products will someday sell in Reynosa, with its burgeoning population of more than a million. Meanwhile, he's planning to keep his day job.

Back home there are a number of isolated villages in the verdant foothills of the Sierra Madre Oriental in northern Veracruz. Generations ago, they were headquarters for large cattle ranches. Few have a population of more than 5,000. Most have weekly open-air markets where farmers and a variety of vendors from throughout the region sell their wares.

For more than 10 years, Carlos set up shop in a tarp-covered stall and spent his Sundays, mostly idle while awaiting a sale or two. So did a dozen other boot makers by the name of Rodriguez. On Wednesdays and Fridays they'd meet again in another town. The customers who frequented the markets, however, bought fruits and produce and maybe a live chicken or two. Most already had a decent pair of boots.

Carlos was a good craftsman. He was proud to say his boots were the best. But he realized he was wasting his time each week. He could have been at home honing his skills, and producing quality leather goods.

Once a friend suggested that the Rodriguez guys from Tantoyuca ought to form a company, or a co-op of some sort to more efficiently produce and market their products. That way one Rodriguez could handle market day while the others were at home working. Perhaps that way they could build up their product line and extend their reach to more distant and more lucrative markets.

No, resounded the chorus of boot-makers That wasn't the way their grandfathers did it. They made a pair of boots, and then they set out to sell them. Besides, some Rodriguezes were better leather craftsmen than others. Some were better salesmen. Some weren't the best of friends.

Carlos' family was growing up fast. His eldest daughter was going to be 15 the following year. That meant he would need lots of money to help celebrate her "*quinceañera*," the most important fiesta in the life of a teenage girl. Impoverished Mexican families set aside their last peso for this traditional rite. In cattle country this called for a "*barbacoa*," the literal slaughtering of a fatted calf, for a village feast. A *quinceañera* done right might set him back $500 or so. Carlos' leather business often struggled to provide an occasional chicken on the table

Then Carlos learned that his wife was pregnant with their fourth child. She had earned a teaching degree, and was hoping to land a classroom position in Tantoyuca. But now her hopes were on hold.

Carlos was 38, and after nearly half his life working in a leather shop in the converted living room of his house he had nothing to show for it. He couldn't pay for his daughter's party and he couldn't afford another child. He was despondent. He started to drink, and stay out late, and one night he met a couple of friends in a bar.

Over a few beers, they talked of getting out of Tantoyuca and starting a new life. They remembered hearing of one guy who made it to the United States and got a good job, and a nice car, and now he was sending home lots of money.

Not very many people had ever left Tantoyuca. Millions of Mexicans had moved to the U.S., but they didn't come from remote, family-centered villages in the Sierra Madre Oriental mountains. Some moved to the big cities, like Tampico and Monterrey and Veracruz and Mexico City, for awhile, but most soon returned to their small-town roots.

Carlos' younger sister took a job as a servant for a wealthy Mexico City couple and later served as a nanny for their son's family during their two-year stay in the United States. She was the first person from Tantoyuca to live in the U.S.

Carlos wasn't ready to make that big of a move quite yet. After all, he had a wife and three children and another on the way. But he knew he had to get out of Tantoyuca. At least for awhile. He had to find a job. He had to make some money.

His friend suggested they check out those jobs with American companies up on the border. The newspapers extolled the billions in revenues and the million jobs that had changed the landscape of the northern border cities. There were modern factories planted in groomed industrial parks on the outskirts of such Rio Bravo cities such as Matamoros, Reynosa and Ciudad Juárez.

Carlos' drinking buddies that night were a couple of bachelors in their early 20s. They had traveled to the border cities. Once they even flirted with the idea of illegally crossing into the United States. They also knew of a friend from a neighboring village who had gone to work in one of the border cities' *maquiladoras*.

As fate would have it, their friend was in town a week later, extolling the opportunities on the frontier. New assembly plants were sprouting up in ever-expanding industrial parks in Reynosa, he said. He had been trained in computers, and had landed a high-tech job that paid double the Mexican minimum wage. And, yes, the American company was looking for new workers, he added.

Carlos' wife wasn't happy with the news. Still, she realized more and more husbands had to leave the village to find work. Some wives followed, but most opted to stay behind in the tranquil towns of their birth, creating a lot of single moms and fatherless families.

Carlos assured her that the job was temporary. He needed to earn some steady money to pay for the new baby and his eldest daughter's *quinceañera.* He'd be gone only a year, perhaps. Besides, Reynosa was just an eight-hour drive away. If he got an extra day off, he might be able to go home on an occasional weekend.

The three were hired by Fisher Hamilton, a U.S. manufacturer of stainless steel cabinetry. The company was new to the Villa Florida industrial park, but its early successes had spurred plans for expansion. About 300 Mexicans were on the payroll, about the same number who had been laid off at the company's plant in Two Rivers, Wisconsin.

Carlos was selected to be trained to run a computer-driven work station which laser-cut and shaped steel sheets for cabinets. He didn't know anything about computers. He never made it to high school. He was a boot-maker and the cutting and shaping and sewing was all done by hand.

He was paid $1 an hour at the start, and got a quarter raise at the end of three months, and another quarter before the end of the year. He especially prized the benefits: free breakfasts and lunches in the company cafeteria each day, free medical care, including physicals and medicines prescribed by a physician in residence, and housing near the plant.

The three men from northern Veracruz pooled their money to pay the rent of the two-room apartment, for food, and for gas for Carlos' 1972 Ford. When their day's off coincided, they'd set off for Tantoyuca for the weekend.

But these days that doesn't happen often. Carlos goes months without seeing his wife and kids, especially since he started to sell his leather products in the Reynosa market on Sundays. But he did save enough of his pay to afford a fancy *quinceañera* fiesta for his daughter and a baptism ceremony for his baby girl.

Carlos now is in his second year of working in the *maquiladora.* He misses his family, but he's gotten used to earning a steady paycheck. But as he hears rumors of more *maquilas* closing and moving their operations to China to save even more in labor costs, he's worried that his days in Reynosa may be numbered.

If he were to lose his job, he doesn't know what he'd do. His buddies told him that if the plant closed, they'd head north across the Rio Bravo. But they weren't married. They didn't have a wife and four kids in Tantoyuca.

Still, Carlos thought aloud, if he were to get a good job in the U.S., he would be able to send a lot more money back home.

# Chapter Four

## *Maquiladoras -2*

✦

### *Foreign factories mean one million jobs*

The Mexican border bustles with business.

It's not just souvenirs and cheap goods and nightlife for the border hopping American tourists. Those were the olden days, before the *maquiladoras*, long before American companies hopped the border in search of cheap labor.

Today the frontier is filled with factories just a stone's throw from the Rio Bravo.

It's also filled with shanties and slums as thousands upon thousands of Mexicans from the interior, many of them small farmers who were pushed off their land by NAFTA and those subsidized, imported grains from the U.S., travel north in search of a job.

For tens of thousands, the *maquilas* offer a glimmer of hope, a paycheck to buy food -- once produced on their land -- to feed their families. For tens of thousands of others, the border is only a short stopover in the journey for a better life in the U.S.

The *maquilas*, cursed by labor but loved by management, are a phenomenon that's not likely to disappear anytime soon. However, they do change their stripes as companies forego any sense of national allegiance for still cheaper labor in parts of Central America and Asia.

In fact, while there now are more than one million workers in Mexican *maquilas*, those numbers are declining as peasants in China settle for $2 a day to work in foreign-owned factories.

The year 2000 was the peak for Mexican *maquilas*. Since then hundreds of *maquilas* have shut down and investment in assembly plants has substantially decreased.

Some of the companies were in residence for less than a decade before they closed up shop and moved on to cheaper labor lands.

When the factories were suddenly shuttered and their operations were moved overseas, thousands of Mexicans were left without a job and without hope on the border. They couldn't go home. Their farms were gone. But they had to feed their families, somehow.

So they headed north – across the river, across the desert. They had no documents but they were desperate. They had friends and relatives in the U.S. They'd help them find a job.

The Spanish term *"maquiladora"* refers to the ancient practice of millers charging a *"maquila"* for processing other farmers' grain. On the Mexican frontier, it now refers to foreign companies profiting greatly by paying a relative pittance in labor costs for product assembly.

A Mexican often earns less than $1 per hour for the same job for the same company that pays $20 per hour in the United States.

Foreign companies are recruited to build modern plants in landscaped industrial parks not far from the U.S. frontier. They import materials and equipment on a duty-free basis for assembly or manufacturing and then ship the assembled product back to the U.S.

Each day hundreds of 18-wheelers cross NAFTA-dedicated bridges linked to the industrial parks loaded with materials. Each day hundreds of trucks head north loaded with finished products for U.S markets.

There are other foreign corporations, from Europe and Japan and Korea, that take advantage of the low-wage *maquilas*, but American companies dominate the industrial parks.

The Border Industrialization Program has been around since the late 1960s when Mexico started to get serious about attracting foreign investment. The *maquilas* got off to a slow start, but by 1985 they accounted for Mexico's second largest source of income from foreign exports, only behind oil.

When the North American Free Trade Agreement went into effect in 1994, investments in Mexico's frontier soared. Between 1995 and 2000, exports of assembled products in Mexico tripled, and the rate of the industry's growth amounted to about one factory per day.

By the end of the century, the industry accounted for 25% of Mexico's gross domestic product and 17% of the total Mexican employment.

Globalization has fueled competition for low-cost labor and since the year 2000 Mexico has lost more than 500 firms that moved their operations to such off-shore stations as Taiwan, China and countries in Central America.

Despite the decline, there still exist more than 3,000 *maquilas* in Mexico, employing more than one million workers. More than $51 billion in supplies have been imported into Mexico and as of 2006, *maquilas* still accounted for 45% of Mexico's exports.

Since profits generated from *maquilas* are sent back to the U.S. or other investor-based countries, the industry does not promote direct economic development within Mexico. Nor does Mexico profit from the imported machinery, which is essentially duty free. Raw materials and parts are exempt from taxes for the first 18 months. They must leave the country as finished goods in that time period.

All the major Mexican cities along the 2,000-mile-long U.S.-Mexico border are home to international companies. Tijuana, across the border from San Diego, CA, hosted the most *maquilas* back in 2001, with 821 companies, although today the number is closer to 550. Ciudad Juárez, across the Rio Grande from El Paso, Texas, at one time had the largest "twin plant" labor force with about 250,000 workers in more than 300 *maquilas*.

But of all the *maquiladora* communities, only Reynosa, across the border from McAllen, Texas, has registered gains both in new industries and in employment. Recruiters based in McAllen say their success stems from the high-tech companies they seek.

The McAllen Economic Development Corp. claims it's created at least 60,000 jobs on the Mexican side. It continues to recruit selected U.S. firms to set up shop in one of Reynosa's 10 spacious industrial parks that now cover 2,730 acres. In terms of plants and number of workers, Reynosa falls far short of Tijuana or Ciudad Juárez. But it's still growing.

Reynosa is the third largest city on the border, with an official population of about 500,000. About 100,000 of those work in the *maquiladoras*. Two-thirds were born in Reynosa. The others, mostly from the state of Veracruz, moved in for the jobs.

They help make plasma TVs, palm pilots, GPS systems, heart catherization kits, auto parts, power tools and even toilets. Among others, they work for Panasonic, GE, Black and Decker, Bissell, Brunswick and Kohler.

Most earn about $6.50 a day, compared to about $120 a day for the average American worker in the same company plant. Most belong to the CTM union that is considered very favorable to industry. There hasn't been a strike or labor conflict since the mid-1980s.

Location, of course, is a critical component of success, and Reynosa is well-positioned at the crossroads of one of the largest Foreign Trade Zones.

Out of the $150 billion in trade that crosses through the south Texas border, almost 40% passes through the Rio Grande Valley.

There are two bridges crossing the river and a third, a four-lane highway dedicated to *maquila* truck traffic, is under construction. It will be linked to the future U.S. Interstate 69 corridor to Canada as well as to the NAFTA highway to Mexico City.

There are no guarantees in the global economy, of course, but Reynosa is positioned better than most border cities to retain its companies and workforce. Those most likely to move to another off-shore location offer routine assembly jobs and have products which have low transportation costs.

Overall, more than a quarter of the *maquilas* in Mexico have had garment and textile operations. About 16% focused on electronics and about 10% were involved in furniture assembly.

The companies get major tax breaks, with a corporate income tax of less than 7% and a nominal real estate tax on their industrial properties. They do have to pay into Mexico's socialized medical system, as well as social security, severance pay, paid holidays, mandatory bonuses and childcare.

The fully loaded wage rate, including fringe benefits, for a new unskilled *maquila* laborer is about $2.30 an hour.

While that pay is less that 10% of the employer's cost in the U.S., millions of Mexicans still earn less than $1 a day.

The *maquiladora* success story is not without social costs. The border populations have exploded as peasants, forced off their farms, leave their families behind to seek work in the factories.

The population of Ciudad Juárez jumped by 50% in a decade to well over 1.2 million. Tin shacks, packing crates and tarpaper hovels shelter workers and the jobless. Vast slums without electricity, running water or sanitary sewers have sprouted up along rutted paths. Municipal services can't keep up with the growth. Juárez also is said to have the worst air pollution on the border.

Rivers and streams are littered with debris and pollutants, as well as toxic waste. The New River, which flows from Mexicali to the Salton Sea in California claims the title of the "dirtiest river in America." One study reported that all streams and rivers in the border region have been adversely affected by the *maquila* industry.

A two-nation accord says hazardous waste generated by U.S. corporations must be transported back to the United States for disposal, but few companies comply with the rule. The U.S. Environmental Protection Agency reported that only 91 of the 600 *maquilas* located on the Texas-Mexico border have returned waste to the U.S. since 1987.

The companies avoid paying disposal costs by dumping toxins and other waste into Mexican rivers and deserts.

The once friendly, sleepy, border towns now are tense, rife with crime. Visitors are given advisories to stay in established tourist areas and then only during daylight hours. The drug cartels have moved their operations to the border, closer to their ultimate customers in the U.S., and rival gangs have taken their bloody battles to the streets.

Most of the *maquila* assembly workers are women, although more men have been recent hires in high-tech and heavy industry fields.

Some assembly plants have been accused of discrimination of women of child-bearing age in order to keep costs down because of Mexico's labor laws and extensive maternity benefits. They often demand pregnancy tests as a prerequisite to employment.

The main goal of the Border Industrialization Program, and its *maquiladora* counterpart was to attract foreign investment. For that to continue to happen, Mexican labor has to remain cheap and competitive with other major outsource countries. To keep production high and costs low, many *maquilas* have harsh working environments.

The low wages – a minimum of $6.50 a day to start -- are insufficient to support a family, and the cost of living on the border is significantly higher than in the interior of the country.

All this has contributed to high employee turnover – as high as 80% in some *maquilas*.

And that has led thousands of temporary border dwellers to trek still farther north in search of a better life.

---

## Chapter Four:  MAQUILADORAS: Among the sources cited:

Scott Carrier, National Public Radio, "Life around the maquiladoras of Juárez," July 5, 2004.

M.J. Hennigan, The Arizona Daily Star, Tucson, AZ, "Maquiladoras in global squeeze," Sept. 3, 2009.

Maquiladora Management Services, San Diego, CA, "Made in Mexico, Inc." 2008.

Wikipedia, "Legal requirements of a maquiladora," 2008.

Columbia Encyclopedia, Columbia University Press,  "Maquiladoras," 2009.

William C. Gruben, Federal Reserve Bank of Dallas, "NAFTA and maquiladoras," June 2001.

Team NAFTA, Reynosa Industrial Profile, 2006.

Tyche Hendricks, San Francisco Chronicle, "On the border: maquiladoras," Nov. 27, 2005.

Matt Rosenburg, About.com, "Maquiladoras in Mexico," 2008.

U.S. Border Patrol vehicles are a familiar sight along the paths and roadways on the frontier. The agency's numbers have been greatly bolstered as part of the border enforcement program. This photo shows the monitored trail along the Rio Grande in Brownsville.

# Chapter Five

## *Amnesty – 1*

◆

### *Victoria brothers' restaurants thrive*

The Brothers Victoria are doing quite well these days. They once were dishwashers. Now they own restaurants. They barely made it through fifth grade. Their kids are college grads.

They once were "illegal aliens." Now they're U.S. citizens. And they're poor no more.

It's been more than 20 years since they had to worry about being picked up by immigration officials and deported to Mexico. Those were the days when every time they went to visit their family in a small village in Michoacán, they had to pay a *coyote* to get back into the United States.

Cresencio Victoria was the first of four brothers to leave La Estancia for the U.S. back in 1973. He was 14 at the time. His uncle Rafael was a dishwasher at a restaurant called "Two Guys from Italy" in downtown Los Angeles. He put up $300, contracted a smuggler, and Rafael got his nephew a job in the kitchen washing pots and pans.

"Chris" still remembers that frightful first trip to the U.S. He spent a month in Tijuana before he finally made it across the border. His groups were stopped three times by the U.S. Border Patrol and sent south. Finally, on the fourth try, Chris made it all the way to Los Angeles. He winces as he tells of the adventure with 20 Mexicans stuffed into the trunk and back seat of a Ford LTD.

And yes, he knew of those who didn't make it. Some drowned in the sewers of Tijuana, others baked in car trunks when the drivers fled authorities. The horror stories of so many migrants were all too true, Chris said.

Yet his family kept coming. Chris saved $300 and bought a *coyote* for his big brother Raymundo, who was 18 at the time. It took him three tries to cross the border. Then it was Ray's turn to buy a *coyote* for brother Noel. And the following year, "Noe" paid the bill for Isidro, better known as "Sid."

All of them got their start washing dishes at "Two Guys from Italy," a franchise with 75 Italian restaurants, mainly on the West Coast. By 1980, the Victoria brothers had learned the ropes of Italian cooking, and were looking for an opportunity to set out on their own.

Their uncle was selected to run a franchise in Salt Lake City, so they lived in Utah for awhile. Chris then helped Rafael set up another restaurant in Dallas. It was there that he found out there was an opening in a place called Wausau. They had never been to the Midwest, but the brothers agreed it would be another adventure, so they packed up the van and headed for Wisconsin.

They operated that franchise from 1981 to 1985. Both Chris and Sid married American women, had a couple of kids and had thoughts of settling down.

But through the grapevine, they had heard of an opportunity in Appleton, Wisconsin, about 100 miles to the east of Wausau. They drove to the Fox Valley to check it out, had their American wives sign the mortgages, and they finally had a restaurant in their own name.

"Victoria's" was an immediate success on College Avenue in downtown Appleton. Few customers were ever aware that the popular Italian restaurant was being run by four illegal aliens from Mexico. Although the brothers craved Mexican specialties when they were back in the kitchen, they only had Italian dishes on the menu.

Within a few years, the restaurant was taking in nearly $900,000 a year, an astronomical amount for four poor boys from Michoacán. Chris recalls joking with his brothers that if they could sell the place, they could go back to Mexico as very rich men.

But Chris had the American dream in mind ever since he was 10 years old. He wasn't about to go back. Besides, by this time, almost every one of his family was in the U.S.

In 1986, the U.S. Congress passed and President Ronald Reagan signed the Immigration Control and Reform Act that granted amnesty to more than three million undocumented immigrants, including 2.3 million Mexicans.

The Victoria brothers were tiring of traveling back and forth from Mexico as fugitives. They were making good money, but they still had to hire *coyotes* to get across the border.

Ray especially wanted a "green card" so he could travel to visit his wife who had remained in La Estancia. He still had burn scars on his stomach from his last *coyote* trip from Mexico. He was the bottom man next to the exhaust pipe in a stack of illegal migrants traveling in a rusty pickup truck.

Chris and Sid wanted to take their American wives and their kids to visit Mexico, but they weren't looking forward to returning to the U.S. in the trunk of some *coyote's* car.

Noe had secured a temporary residence card back in 1978, but the other brothers had no legal documents.

Still, they were so busy at the restaurant that they didn't file an application for amnesty and start the process toward "green card" permanent residency until the last week of the program in May 1988. They were among 47 illegal aliens who filed for temporary U.S. residency through the Green Bay Catholic Diocesan Refugee, Migration and Hispanic Service.

After more than 15 years of living, working and traveling in the U.S. with a illegal cloud hovering over his head, Chris was legal at last. So were three of his brothers. His youngest brother, Alex, was born in Los Angeles and thus was the first U.S. citizen in the family. His two sisters married Mexicans who were permanent U.S. residents. His father and mother got "green cards." More than a dozen nieces and nephews were born in the U.S.A.

The Victoria family dynasty took off soon after the illegal veil was lifted. Chris opened another restaurant in Green Bay, and one in Oshkosh, and added yet another one in both Green Bay and Appleton. At one time there were four Victoria's in the Fox Valley, and the restaurants took in more than $4 million a year.

Chris admitted "going a little crazy" with expansion plans, and suddenly having no time for his family. "I became too American," he said. "It was work, work, work, and dreams of becoming a millionaire."

So he closed two of the restaurants, and concentrated on the original Appleton and Green Bay operations, cutting the total take in half. "But now I'm enjoying life a million times more," he said.

Family is sacred to the Victorias. Chris' two sisters live in Minneapolis and take care of their 85-year-old father who suffered a stroke and is paralyzed. Their mother Soledad is 75, and lives with Chris. She's still an integral part of the family business, working seven days a week, laundering napkins and tablecloths.

"We Latinos take care of our elderly," Chris said. "We don't put them in nursing homes."

Chris confesses that his marriage to Wendy just didn't work out. His two grown sons, Cresencio Jr., 23, and Miguel 21, however, make their father proud.

Cresencio graduated from a fashion design school in New York City and is currently teaching English in Taiwan, as well as learning Chinese to prepare for a career in New York. Miguel is a senior majoring in business at the University of Wisconsin-Oshkosh. In his spare time, he's a waiter at Victoria's. Someday, he hopes to take over the business.

Chris' wife Lizett, daughter of Mexican immigrants from Sonora, was born in Los Angeles. They have three young children, a girl aged 9 and two boys, ages 6 and 4. He admits that these days he enjoys the kids more than the restaurant.

Chris met Lizett at his mother's house. Back in Los Angeles, Soledad ran a childcare center and Lizett became part of that family from an early age. When she graduated from high school, Lizett contacted Soledad in Appleton and asked to stay with her while she went on to college and found a job.

Chris and Ray today run the Appleton restaurant, Noe manages the Green Bay operation, Sid is in Rochester, Minnesota, and Alex owns a restaurant in Minneapolis.

Chris remembers working in the strawberry fields of La Estancia when he was barely 10 years old. He also recalls listening intently to his grandfather's tales of his time in the big cities and fertile valleys of California. His grandfather was a *bracero*, a contracted laborer, who hoed vegetables in the Imperial Valley and picked oranges upstate.

Chris' father was a *bracero*, too. The U.S. first issued permits to Mexicans who were contracted by growers to ease worker shortages during World War II. However, the program did continue until 1964.

His father was in California for about six months every year during the growing and harvesting seasons. Then he would return to the family's subsistence farm in La Estancia where his U.S. wages would carry them over until the next season. Even after the *bracero* program ended, his father often sneaked back in the U.S. to weed and harvest the crops.

It wasn't a bad life, but Chris wanted a better one. He knew he was on his way to the U.S. long before he finished fifth grade. But he wasn't going to work in the fields of California and he surely wasn't going to pick strawberries when he returned to La Estancia. His village, in the Tziróndaro Valley, wasn't far from Zamora de Hidalgo, a city of 100,000 or so, but it just didn't have the appeal of Los Angeles.

Chris hasn't been back to La Estancia for a number of years. He's been too busy running restaurants and raising two families. But he remembers well his past and he's sympathetic to the plight of the Mexican migrants who have flooded across the U.S. border in the past two decades seeking work.

He's hired a number of Mexicans at his restaurants over the years, taking care to see that they have legal documents. However, he realizes that some of them do have falsified papers.

He remembers one Saturday evening when his restaurant was crowded with patrons from all over the country, and two men wearing U.S. Border Patrol uniforms walked in the front door.

The receptionist hollered, "*Migras, migras!*" And every waiter, cook and dishwasher scurried out the back doors. No one was left inside to serve the customers.

Chris at the time was on the restaurant's roof, checking an exhaust fan, when he saw a dozen employees sprinting across the street. "*Muchachos*, where are you going?" he yelled in Spanish. The workers, believing an immigration raid was underway and that Chris was another officer, raced into a church parking lot, seeking sanctuary.

The two Border Patrol officers were assigned to the northern frontier with Canada, and they had been in the region to put on a demonstration of drug-sniffing dogs for those attending the annual Experimental Aircraft Association's convention in Oshkosh. The event draws hundreds of thousands of aviation enthusiasts from throughout the world.

There was no raid. But the restaurant manager that evening was taking no chances. When he saw the Border Patrol vehicle parked in front of his house, he went in the back door, got his family and moved into the Paper Valley Hotel down the block for the night.

The "raid" set off the migrant alert network. Chris said he fielded telephone calls from all over, as far away as Minneapolis, asking about the Border Patrol's invasion.

Chris now can smile about the incident. It's humorous, but it's also tragic. So many Mexican immigrants now are in the shadows living in fear of the day when they might lose their jobs, have their families split up, spend time behind bars and face deportation.

Chris senses that many Americans are opposed to reforming U.S. immigration policies. But he insists the system has to be fixed. Mexicans don't come to the U.S. to be on welfare, but rather to work. "So let them work," he says, noting that many of his waiters are working two jobs.

Mexicans are doing jobs that most Americans don't want to do, Chris said, pointing to the meatpacking and dairy farming industries in Wisconsin, now dominated by Latino immigrants.

He sees a simple solution to the contentious immigration issue, not unlike the *bracero* program that drew his grandfather and his father to the U.S. a half-century ago. If the U.S. needs workers, it should issue permits. If it doesn't, it shouldn't.

The ones who get in trouble, throw them out, Chris says. The ones who behave, keep them.

# Chapter Five

## *Amnesty – 2*

✦

### *1.9 million Mexicans legalized in 1986*

On Nov. 6, 1986, after 34 years with no major immigration legislation, and six long years of trying to send an acceptable bill through both houses of Congress, President Ronald Reagan signed into law the Immigration Reform and Control Act.

It was better known as the amnesty act.

The act amended the Immigration and Nationality Act of 1952, and it was aimed to better control unauthorized immigration, which many in Congress insisted had gotten out of control. More than one-third of the U.S. population growth that year was attributed to immigration.

The legislation, also known as the Simpson-Mazzoli Act for its Congressional sponsors, was endorsed by a bipartisan Commission on Immigration Reform, chaired by the Rev. Theodore Hesburgh, C.S.C., then president of the University of Notre Dame.

Three million "illegal aliens," including 2.3 million Mexicans, were given the opportunity to become legal residents. The conditions were simple. They had to have lived five years in the U.S., have no serious criminal record, tested negative for HIV virus and have at least a minimal understanding and knowledge of the English language along with U.S. history and government.

They also could apply for U.S. citizenship five years after they received permanent resident status, or "green cards."

Those "illegals" who did not apply for residence could no longer remain in the U.S. and adjust to permanent resident status unless they were immediate relatives of U.S. citizens.

A total of 2.7 million undocumented immigrants were granted amnesty by the time the program ended in 1988. A total of 85% were from Latin America; 70% were Mexicans.

There were two categories of eligible immigrants. The "legally authorized workers" numbered 1.7 million. The "special agriculture workers" numbered about 1.1 million. The latter category gave rise to massive immigration fraud charges as officials had estimated that only 400,000 SAW immigrants would be eligible.

More than half of all the newly legalized immigrants resided in California six years later, causing a backlash that led to the adoption of the anti-immigrant Proposition 187.

Not all of the undocumented applied for amnesty. Only 60% to 70% of the qualified immigrants came forward and were legalized. There was fear among the illegal aliens that amnesty was a trick designed to fool them into revealing themselves so they could be deported.

When the grace period ended in 1988, there were an estimated four million illegal aliens still living in the U.S.

Amnesty was only part of the IRCA legislation. It was mainly an effort to greatly reduce the number of illegals already in the U.S. But it also promised to make it tougher on future undocumented immigrants.

The principal target of IRCA was the employer. The Act called for sanctions against companies that knowingly hired illegal aliens. It was a civil penalty for the first offense but it became a criminal penalty for repeat offenders. There were loopholes, however, to appease the employers. There was an "affirmative defense" clause that freed employers from checking the authenticity of the workers' documents.

Agricultural employers increased their lobbying efforts for more temporary worker programs, and that shifted the focus away from hiring sanctions.

Employers also got around IRCA's potential sanctions by turning the hiring process over to subcontractors. By using a subcontractor, the workers weren't employees and thus the employer wasn't liable.

The year IRCA was signed, the number of undocumented Mexicans crossing the border declined. But soon it rebounded to "normal" levels. By 1990 there were a million more Mexicans living in the U.S.

In the 1990 census, there were an estimated 3.5 million illegal immigrants in the U.S. Five years later, the number had surged to 5 million. In the year 2000, it was 8.4 million, and in another five years it had jumped to 11.1 million.

There were extenuating circumstances that caused millions of people to leave their lands and enter illegally into the U.S. over the past two decades. But by any measure, the amnesty program did not live up to its promises of halting illegal immigration.

Mexican migrants have been crossing the frontier long before there was any semblance of a border. Back in the 1840s, most of the American southwest belonged to Mexico. When the U.S. annexed 500,000 square miles of Mexican land, equivalent in size to all of Western Europe, it also annexed 100,000 Mexicans and 200,000 Native Americans living there.

Between 1850 and 1880, some 55,000 Mexican workers emigrated to the U.S. to become field hands in the very regions that had belonged to Mexico a couple of decades earlier. Then came the railroad in 1890 and 60% of the crews were Mexican.

Ever since those pioneer days, the United States relationship with its southern neighbor has been schizophrenic. When it needs Mexicans, it recruits them. When it doesn't, it deports them.

While Europe was sending millions of its citizens across the Atlantic Ocean to the U.S., Mexicans were content to stay home. In 1900, when the U.S. population topped 76 million, only about 500,000 were Hispanics

No one fretted about immigration on the southern border, except for the Chinese who were trying to sneak into the U.S. through Mexico. In fact, some Mexicans, the ancestors of today's *coyotes*, taught the Chinese to speak Spanish and wear sombreros so they could pass for Mexicans at the border.

Before Mexican workers bailed out American agriculture, it was the Chinese who filled the labor hole. Nearly 200,000 Chinese were legally contracted to cultivate California fields – until the Chinese Exclusion Act of 1882.

The Immigration Act of 1917 was the first legislation aimed at Mexican immigrants. It called for a literacy test and an $8 head tax, but those provisions were soon waived as World War I broke out and a U.S. labor shortage created the first "*bracero*" program. Mexicans were recruited by "*enganchadores*" to work in the fields of California.

The Mexican Revolution of 1911-1929 killed one million Mexicans and sent another million north to the U.S. Many later returned to their country.

Then along came the Great Depression. While Mexicans had been welcomed a decade earlier, the public response now had changed. Visas were denied to all Mexicans who failed to prove they had secure employment in the U.S. Between 1929 and 1935, the U.S. forcefully expelled 415,000 Mexicans. Another 85,000 left voluntarily. In total, more than one million Mexicans, including tens of thousands of U.S. citizens of Mexican descent, were deported.

The Mexican work force was critical in developing the economy and prosperity of the U.S. And every time the U.S. found a reason to close the door on Mexican immigration, an historic event would force them to reopen that door.

In 1942, the U.S. once again needed Mexican labor. World War II had decimated the work force. The government created the "*bracero*" program and reopened the floodgates for legal immigration of Mexican workers. More than four million Mexican farm workers were contracted with U.S. growers and ranchers before the program ended in 1964.

But long before that year, there were a number of efforts to get Mexicans out of the country.

At the end of World War II, many Mexican workers were ousted from their jobs by returning servicemen. In 1947, the Emergency Farm Labor Service set out to cut the amount of imported labor from Mexico. In the decade that ended in 1954, there was a major surge of illegal immigrants from Mexico.

In 1954, before "Operation Wetback" got underway, more than one million workers had crossed the Rio Grande illegally. The roundup of illegals was orchestrated by the U.S. government in response to public hysteria about the growing number of Mexican immigrants.

The U.S. Border Patrol, assisted by municipal, county, state and federal authorities, began a quasi-military operation of search and seizure of all illegal immigrants, starting in the lower Rio Grande Valley and moving north. Before "Operation Wetback" was over, as many as 1.3 million Mexicans were deported.

The roundup of illegals came to an end after U.S. citizens of Mexican descent complained of police stopping all "Mexican looking" people. They accused authorities of using extreme "police-state" methods, including deportation of American-born children who by law were U.S. citizens.

By the 1960s, an overflow of illegal agriculture workers along with the invention of the mechanical cotton harvester, diminished the practicality and appeal of the *bracero* program. Those events, along with the violations of *bracero* employers who favored lower-cost illegals, brought the program to an end in 1964.

In 1965, the U.S. Congress passed the Immigration and Nationality Act Amendments that abolished the system of national-origin quotas. The number of legal immigrants surged, from 2.5 million in the 1950s to 4.5 million in the 1970s; to 7.3 million in the 1980s; to 10 million in the 1990s.

In the early 2000s, one million legal immigrants were added to the population each year. That number included 600,000 "change of status" immigrants who already were in the U.S.

The number of illegal immigrants also soared during that period, with 130,000 per year in the 1970s jumping to 300,000 in the 1980s; to 500,000 per year in the 1990s; and to more than 700,000 per year in the early 2000s.

Illegal immigrants, 3.5 million in the wake of the 1986 amnesty act, had grown to more than 12 million.

The word "amnesty" had become vilified. It didn't do what it was supposed to. "Legalization" became the term more politically correct.

In 2001 President George W. Bush proposed giving legal residency to as many as four million Mexicans. The scheme was endorsed by Mexican President Vincente Fox. But Bush could hardly get a second to the motion from his fellow Republicans. They were haunted by the specter of the failed amnesty legislation of 1986.

Yet, on the 20th anniversary of Senate Bill 1200, Congress was faced with Senate Bill 2611, another go-around over legalizing illegal aliens. This time it's called the Hagel-Martinez bill, and it's akin to the Simpson-Mazzoli bill.

Except the stakes are much higher.

Nearly 10 million illegal aliens now would be in line for legalization. The bill also would allow an estimated 4.5 million family members to join their legalized relatives, raising the total to 14.5 million new legal immigrants.

There are three categories of immigrants in the bill.

One is for those illegally in the U.S. for five years or more. They would be on a "glide path" to lawful permanent residence. Another is for those in the country from two to five years. They can apply for "deferred mandatory departure" and be part of a guest worker program with a H2C visa. They first have to leave the country. They then can apply for a "green card" after four years. The third category is for those who work in agriculture. They can apply for a "blue card" and then seek lawful permanent residence (LPR) after three to five years.

Critics say the new amnesty bill is fraught with fraud. Supporters insist that new technologies will root out falsified applications. Besides, they say, there will be better enforcement of the law and stiffer penalties for errant employers. And the U.S. Chamber of Commerce, which didn't like the 1986 legislation, supports this bill.

Still, three years after the legalization bill was introduced, it's gone nowhere. That failed 1986 scheme continues to cast a long shadow over the any immigration reform effort that looks like "amnesty."

---

## Chapter Five: AMNESTY: Among the sources cited:

David Simcox, Center for Immigration Studies, "Measuring the fallout of IRCA," May 1997.

Joseph Nevens, "Dying to Live: U.S. immigration in an age of global apartheid," 2008 copyright.

Peter Geniesse, The Post-Crescent, Appleton, WI, "Illegal no longer," May 8, 1988.

Pia M. Orrenius, Federal Reserve Bank of Dallas, "Does amnesty encourage illegal immigration?" 2002.

Public Broadcasting System, "The Border: Mexican Immigrant Labor History," 2008.

Wikipedia, "History of immigration to the United States," 2009.

Rachel L. Swarns, The New York Times, "Failed amnesty of 1986 haunts current bills," May 23, 2006.

Steven A. Camarota, Center for Immigration Studies, "Amnesty under Hagel-Martinez," June 2006.

Some 700 miles of the Mexican border now are behind walls and fences constructed at a cost of more than a billion dollars. The levees along the Rio Grande in Texas were also reconstructed for both surveillance and flood control.

# Chapter Six

## *The Roots – 1*

✦

### *IMF, World Bank take big toll on poor*

Why?

Why did millions of Mexicans leave their homes and families over the past two decades to come to the United States to work menial jobs and be subject to racial smears and abuse?

Why would anyone trek across mountains and deserts, risking his life for a pitiful paycheck, only to be hunted down and jailed for being illegal alien?

Why now? What has caused the unprecedented surge of undocumented Hispanic immigrants?

Few Americans care to entertain the questions and the causes which are key to unlocking the answers to the immigration imbroglio.

Many just prefer to build tall border walls and lots of jails, and round up the 12 million illegals and send them back to wherever they came from. Many conveniently forget their own immigrant roots, except to tout that their ancestors were legal.

Few ever delve into the real roots of migration, the conditions and governmental policies that push and pull people across borders.

There have been numerous migration surges to the United States from Mexico and Latin America over the past century. There have been civil wars and revolutions, devastating earthquakes, floods and droughts, all of which have sent people packing for the north. But nothing compares to the exodus of Latinos over the past 25 years.

A century ago, millions of immigrants came to settle in the U.S. from Europe to seek a better life for their families. But during that period, most of the Mexicans stayed put.

So, why in the 1980s did Mexico start sending their young people on a perilous path to the U.S.?

In the past two decades more than 10% of the Mexico-born population migrated to the U.S., most without legal documents. By 2004, more than 11 million Mexican natives were living in the U.S. Several million more had tried to get in the country, but were turned back at the border – the first time. Other millions had been deported. Still several thousand others had died in the desert en route to the U.S.

The easy answer is jobs. Mexico's population grows by more than one million a year. Fewer than a half-million jobs are created. Thus, a half-million people have to look elsewhere for work. That's the push. The pull is the American dream, the good life, and a wage that is 10 times that earned by a Mexican worker.

The Mexican migration to the U.S. is among the largest flows of people in the world. In one year, 2005, more than 600,000 came to America, joining the 23 million persons of Mexican descent already living in the U.S.

The diaspora could be attributed to failed economic policies that have been unable to generate employment and reduce poverty.

NAFTA could be blamed. Unfair trade policies since 1994 have forced two million farmers off their land, and many now are working the fields north of the border.

But the roots of migration still go much deeper.

Mexico, back in the early 1980s, was in good shape. It was considered an "upper-middle-income" country. It had a gross national product one-third that of the U.S. However, it also had a population growth of 3.5% a year, and the nation was considered to be in a demographic transition.

The oil industry was growing and the economy was humming. For nearly a decade, Mexico recklessly borrowed, based on the inflated prices for oil. When the price of oil crashed in 1982, Mexico suddenly was in serious trouble. It defaulted on its debt payments. It owed huge sums of money to banks in the U.S. and Europe.

In stepped the International Monetary Fund and the World Bank with new loans to rescue the international credit system. Those loans came with conditions, however.

They're known as Structural Adjustment Programs. Mexico had to agree to impose strict economic measures to reschedule their debts or borrow more money.

The goal was to make its economy more competitive and attractive to foreign investors. That meant Mexico had to privatize national industries, cut public services, remove wage and price protection, eliminate tariffs and barriers to trade, and devalue its currency to stimulate exports. It had to take care of its suitors, at the expense of its people.

It was the age of "neo-liberalism," a system based on free enterprise and free trade. It was called *laissez faire* in another era. Neo-liberals are against government intervention in the economy and believe that corporations should have absolute freedom to do business anywhere in the world. They call for eliminating national laws that get in the way of business interests, such as environmental and labor regulations.

The International Monetary Fund and the World Bank both were created in 1944 to help governments rebuild post-war economies. They are separate institutions with distinct roles. The World Bank makes loans for development projects and the IMF lends to governments to make their economies appear stable to the international market. Both are mostly funded and controlled by the U.S. and a handful of other First World nations.

Mexico was required to replace small "staple foods" farms with large-scale export farming. It was encouraged to sell public industries to foreign investors. It had to cut back on food subsidies, permitting prices in the marketplace to soar. It had to eliminate jobs and slash wages for workers in government services. It had to devalue the national currency, lowering export earnings and increasing import costs.

It also was told to spend less on health, education and social services.

Since 1982, the Mexican government has complied with nearly all of the adjustment policies of the IMF and World Bank. The result has been a "trickle-up" process that has concentrated the wealth in the hands of few, and has transferred the control of resources from public to private ownership.

The richest 20% of the population received 54% of the national income in 1992, up from 48% in 1984. The income of the poorest 20% of Mexicans fell from 5% in 1984 to 4.3% of national income in 1992.

One of the world's wealthiest men, Carlos Slim, the owner of Teléfonos de Mexico, was said by Forbes magazine to be worth nearly $14 billion. His assets total roughly twice that of the poorest 20% of the population. That's 20 million people who live in extreme poverty with earnings of less than $350 a year.

During the administration of President Carlos Salinas de Gortari, from 1988 to 1994, the number of billionaires in Mexico rose from two to 24.

The Structural Adjustment Program also has negatively affected small industries and producers who were unprepared for the dropping of trade barriers and were unable to compete with cheap imports. The cost of living has skyrocketed. While the minimum wage has increased by 136% since the 1980s, the cost of a basket of basic goods has soared by 371%.

The cuts in public spending have hurt the poor the most, since health care was encouraged to be private, rather than public, and most couldn't afford the private alternatives.

During the 1980s, the health budget as a percentage of overall public spending fell from 4.7% to 2.7%. One result was that between 1980 and 1992, infant deaths, due to nutritional deficiencies, nearly tripled the rate of the 1970s. With 30,000 such deaths each year, Mexico was near the bottom of the UNICEF's ratings of countries' efforts to address malnutrition.

Mexico witnessed a steep and continual decline in real wages during the 1980s, alongside massive layoffs and high levels of unemployment. The minimum wage, pegged at about $4 a day in the early 1990s, lost 53% of its purchasing power between 1982 and 1988, and another 28% from 1988 to 1994.

A 1991 study indicated that out of an economically active population of 34 million, 15% were unemployed and another 40%, some 14 million people, were underemployed.

That year more than one half of all Mexicans (42 million) lived in poverty, and 18 million lived in conditions of extreme poverty.

After a decade of abiding by the terms of the Structural Adjustment Program, Mexico's rich became ever richer, and its poor, ever so much more desperate, left the land and headed north.

In the 1980s and early 1990s, an estimated 400,000 Mexicans each year migrated to California alone, turning it into the nation's most racially and ethnically diverse state.

At the time the Immigration Reform and Control Act went into effect in 1986, more than three million Mexicans were in the U.S. illegally.

In 1960, less than 6% of the foreign-born nationals in the U.S. were Mexicans. In 1990, that share had soared to more than 21%, or 4.2 million people who were born in Mexico.

World Bank and IMF officials had said that the adjustment's attack on poverty would take time, but 12 years after Mexico signed on to the harsh measures to get out of debt, living conditions for the masses had never been worse, and there was no light at the end of the tunnel.

And that set the stage for NAFTA.

# Chapter Six

## *The Roots – 2*

✦

## *NAFTA exports 10 million Mexicans*

It was New Year's Day, 1994, when the cultures collided.

It was the birthday of the North American Free Trade Agreement, the much- heralded scheme aimed to bring Mexico's citizens and economy into the 21st century.

The milestone was greeted by massive protests in Chiapas, the nation's poorest and most indigenous state, on the Guatemalan frontier.

The Zapatistas, rag-tag insurgents under the direction of a masked man called Subcomandante Marcos, seized several towns and cities in the vicinity of San Cristóbol de las Casas. They sought a public platform to tell the world that Mexico was embarking on a plan that would spell disaster for the indigenous and the poor throughout Mexico.

They feared losing control of their lands. They opposed the neo-liberal globalization policies. They believed that would destroy their peasant way of life.

Mexico sent in its troops the next day, and numerous clashes left at least 65 dead.

Ten days later, a ceasefire was brokered by Catholic Bishop Samuel Ruiz, of the Diocese of San Cristóbol. However, the conflict flared and simmered amid attempts at negotiations over the next decade.

The Zapatista National Liberation Army is named after Emiliano Zapata, a popular hero of the 1910-1917 Mexican revolution, who defended poor peasants' right to free land seized from wealthy landowners.

"We didn't go to war to kill or be killed," Subcomandante Marcos, the charismatic leader who used the Internet to spread the message, declared. "We went to war in order to be heard."

His message was picked up by a wide variety of solidarity groups, and it even was amplified by the U.S. rock band "Rage Against the Machine."

At least one-third of the population of Chiapas is considered indigenous. Some, like the Lacandón, are direct descendants of the Mayan Indians and have been living much like their ancestors did for the past 500 years. Most live off the land, and tend small parcels for growing corn and beans.

Under NAFTA, they feared, their land and their livelihoods would be jeopardized. Crop subsidies would be curtailed, and the peasant farmers would be forced to compete in the marketplace with imported U.S. products that were artificially fertilized, mechanically harvested and genetically modified.

They had good reason to fear for their land and for their future. President Carlos Salinas, in preparation for NAFTA, had already repealed existing agrarian reform legislation in 1992. He allowed communal *ejido* lands to be sold off, rented, or to be dissolved entirely. Land distribution programs were to be discontinued and small farmers were to lose access to credit and state price supports.

The Zapatistas continued to issue warnings, and garnered sympathy throughout Mexico, but they could not derail the North American Free Trade Agreement.

President Salinas hailed NAFTA as Mexico's entry into the First World. He promised that free trade and foreign investment would jump-start the country's development, empowering a richer and more prosperous Mexico "to export goods, not people."

Fifteen years later, Mexico's exports have indeed soared. Both goods and people. Almost a half-million Mexicans headed north of the border in 2008, seeking opportunities in the U.S. that they do not have at home.

NAFTA and Mexico did get off to a bad start. Before it had a chance to prove its worth, the bottom had fallen out of the peso in December 1994, and the "Mexican Meltdown" was on.

President Salinas had borrowed $33 billion in short-term loans to keep his house of cards from crashing down before he left office. He then refused to devalue the over-valued peso, leaving that to his successor, Ernesto Zedillo. When Zedillo took office, the peso's buying power had fallen 40%. When he was forced to devalue on Dec. 20, the financial markets were stunned and the peso sank from three to ten to a dollar overnight.

Panicked investors pulled their money out of the country at a rate of $1.5 billion a day. Capital flight emptied out the nation's once healthy reserves.

Salinas' short-term loans were coming due, and Mexico was staring down default by January 1995.

Farmers, encouraged by the privatized banks, had borrowed beyond their means to position themselves for NAFTA's bonanza, and couldn't cover their loans and now faced foreclosure. Urban borrowers were squeezed by soaring interest rates that topped out at 100%.

By February 1995, Mexico had lurched into its deepest economic slide since the Great Depression.

U.S. President Bill Clinton, recognizing the substantial stake U.S. investors had in Mexico, proposed a $40 billion bailout in loan guarantees. When the U.S. Congress balked, he altered the rescue plan to allow Mexico to dip into the U.S. Treasury Department's "Exchange Stabilization Fund," designed to help America's "friends" out of temporary currency crises. Mexico got $2.5 billion with repayment schedules stretching out to 10 years.

The fallout from the "meltdown" in 1995 affected all segments of society, but it impacted the poor the most. Nearly two million workers lost their jobs as factories and businesses failed or severely cut back production. Unemployment rates more than doubled. Inflation reached nearly 50%. The peso lost half of its value, and the Mexican stock market fell 35% in the first year of NAFTA.

The government only measured urban unemployment. But the jobless problem was much greater in the rural areas. More than one million small farmers were in the process of being forced off their lands. Many of the displaced went north to work in the *maquiladoras* on the Mexican frontier. Even more fled across the border to the U.S. to find work.

From 1995 to 1999, nearly three million undocumented migrants, mostly Mexicans, settled in the U.S.

Remittances, money sent south by Mexican workers in the U.S., became Mexico's second source of dollars, right behind petroleum. One out of every four Mexican families subsisted on the *remesas*.

The cure prescribed for the monetary crisis was the same as proposed by the World Bank and the International Monetary Fund 13 years earlier. NAFTA had locked in the fundamentals of neo-liberalism: an open market; an export-oriented economy; privileges for transnational corporations; withdrawal of the state from social programs to promote development; international labor competition and downward pressure on wages and conditions.

The World Bank, which postured Mexico's Structural Adjustment Program as a model for other nations to emulate just months before the crash, blamed the government for the crisis. It claimed Mexico had failed to implement the last few crucial reforms in its free-market economic program. The IMF insisted the economic collapse had been triggered by the selfish actions of Mexican investors.

Both the World Bank and IMF have shown no interest in examining the relationship between economic adjustment programs and the social and economic problems they have left in their wake.

Critics claim that while those agencies' policies were intended to control inflation and generate foreign exchange to help pay off the debt, they have resulted in increased unemployment, poverty and economic polarization.

"While the World Bank and IMF were applauding Mexico's economic performance under adjustment, one half of the population was living in poverty and their ranks were swelling daily," according to a study by the Development Group for Alternative Policies.

It claimed that by steadily tearing away at Mexico's economic and social fabric – and particularly at the well-being of its small rural and urban producers – the agencies set the stage for the economic collapse of December 1994.

The study concluded: "The case of Mexico is a clear lesson that success in the achievement of some macroeconomic indicators of success does not necessarily translate into the improved social well-being of the population. The pursuit of economic efficiency and short-term profits overrode concerns about greater equity, leading to an increased economic polarization of society."

The debate still rages over NAFTA's costs and benefits to the Mexican – and American -- people, 15 years after it got off to a stumbling start. Many have called for the renegotiation of the agreement, especially as pertains to agricultural trade.

But for better or worse, NAFTA has fostered enormous changes in the economies of Mexico, Canada and the United States that won't go away anytime soon.

It's now the world's largest free trade area, with 439 million people producing $15.3 trillion worth of goods and services annually.

The numbers are staggering. The total trade between the U.S. and its NAFTA partners grew from $293 billion in 1993 to $929 billion in 2007, an increase of 213%.

According to the U.S. Embassy reports, each day the NAFTA partners conduct nearly $2.4 billion in trilateral goods trade, or $1.7 million a minute. U.S. trade in goods with Canada and Mexico in 2006 more than exceeded U.S. trade with the 27 members of the European Union and Japan combined.

The U.S. is Mexico's largest trading partner, buying 82% of Mexican exports in 2007. Mexico is the third largest U.S. trading partner after Canada and China.

U.S. goods exports to Mexico totaled $139 billion in 2007. U.S. goods imports from Mexico were $223 billion the same year.

Mexico is the United States' second largest agricultural trading partner. The U.S. imports were valued at $11 billion in 2007; U.S. exports to Mexico were $13.3 billion.

In the first 10 years of NAFTA, all three countries experienced economic growth of more than 30%.

In that same period, 1.3 million jobs were lost in Mexico's agricultural sector.

The numbers, of course, don't tell the whole story.

Between 1993 and 1998, some 967,000 jobs were created in fixed establishments, with one-third of those jobs in the textiles and clothing sectors, followed by machinery and equipment, including the auto industry, and the food industry. A half-million new *maquila* jobs on the northern frontier were created in the same period.

That sounds impressive until it is noted that the principal Mexican manufacturing growth after the passage of NAFTA took place in *maquiladora* industries, which had been around for 30 years before free trade.

Wages declined by 21% between 1994 and 2000, and combined with bleak jobless figures, that forced people to become street vendors to pay the bills. Those micro-businesses, low-income, unstable activities of fewer than five employees now account for 50% of the non-agricultural jobs in the country.

The scarcity of new jobs and the continued absence of well-paying jobs has contributed to the growing inequality of income in Mexico. Critics label NAFTA's legacy as "high-productivity poverty," and assert that low wages means low purchasing power, hardly a successful strategy for globalization.

Until 1984, there was a movement toward greater equality in income distribution. But then the World Bank's Structural Adjustment Program kicked in, the rich got richer and the poor started a stampede north.

Mexico's economic growth under NAFTA has averaged only about 3% a year, far below what is needed to create jobs for a million young people who enter the work force each year and the millions more who barely scrape by. New economic growth projections for 2009 put the figure at 1.9%, due to the downturn of the U.S. economy.

NAFTA can't be blamed for all of Mexico's economic and social ills. After all, the foundation for today's crisis was laid in the early 1980s when the

IMF and World Bank set out to resolve Mexico's debt. But by incorporating and continuing those neo-liberal economic models, NAFTA has greatly accelerated the problems faced by both the U.S. and Mexico.

Since NAFTA was born on New Year's Day in 1994, some 10 million Mexicans have crossed the U.S. border in search of survival, jobs and a promise of a better life.

During just the administration of President Vincente Fox, from 2000 to 2006, a total of 3.4 million migrants moved to the U.S.

A disproportionate number of those migrants were indigenous from Chiapas who no longer could feed their families, due to the demise of the *ejidos* and NAFTA's agricultural restrictions.

Instead of tilling the land of their fathers, they now work on mega-farms in the U.S., and send back money to their families so they can buy American corn and beans in their markets.

The Zapatistas were proven prophetic.

---

## Chapter Six: ROOTS: Among the resources cited:

Carlos Heredia, Development Group for Alternative Policies, "Structural Adjustment in Mexico," 1995.

International Monetary Fund, "IMF Lending: A fact sheet," March 2009.

Juanita Darling, Los Angeles Times, "Mexican revolt in 2nd day; 65 dead," Jan. 3, 1994.

Elisabeth Malkin, The New York Times, "Nafta's promise, unfulfilled," March 24, 2009.

U.S. Embassy, Mexico City, Public Affairs, "NAFTA: U.S.- Mexico at a glance," September 2008.

John Ross, North American Congress on Latin America, "Memories of the Meltdown," Oct. 8, 2008.

Gale Encyclopedia of U.S. Economic History, "Mexican Bail-out," July 2009.

Carlos Salas, NACLA Report on the Americas, "Mexico's haves and have-nots," February 2002.

Laura Carlsen, Center for International Policy, "Armoring NAFTA: Battleground for Mexico's future," Sept. 19, 2008.

The Mexican military has been called upon to quell domestic disturbances as well as serve as the front line in the campaign against the drug cartels. The federal police, in this photo, monitored a small political demonstration in full riot gear in Mexico City's zócolo.

# Chapter Seven

## *Militarization – 1*

✦

### *Mexico's army called in to squelch protests*

It was a sunny, tranquil day in Mexico City's Zócolo. Scores of tourists, vendors, peasants and politicians were milling about one of the world's largest city plazas. If the stones could speak, they'd tell of Hernán Cortés and how the Spaniards covered up the grandest set of temples and palaces of the Aztec Empire.

Mass was underway in the massive Metropolitan Cathedral, one of the first buildings constructed by *Conquistadores* in the 1520s, right on top of that Aztec site. Visitors were standing in awe of the antiquity of the Templo Mayor ruins nearby, the very spot where legend has it that the Aztecs saw an eagle with a snake in its beak, perched on a cactus.

That was the symbol they sought where to build their dynasty. It remains the symbol of Mexico.

Over at the National Palace, on the east side of the zócolo, it was government business as usual. Mexico's president today commands the same site as Moctezuma II did in the early 16th century.

It was just after noon on a Monday in February 2009 when the plaza suddenly came alive. Loudspeakers atop a pickup truck blared an indistinguishable message along with cacophonic music as a group of demonstrators filed their way into the Plaza de la Constitución. They waved banners and shouted slogans.

But they weren't the main attraction. In an instant, a company of federal police, in full riot gear with helmets, face masks, fiberglass shields and wielding batons, was in formation, six deep, in front of the National Palace. They were called to attention by their commander and their steely eyes were fixed on the demonstrators.

The federal police numbered about 120. The demonstrators, a rag-tag group in support of a local political candidate, numbered perhaps 30. It took them about 10 minutes to cross the plaza, and the two sides never got closer than a city block. There was no confrontation.

Then the commander gave the dismissal order and the riot police filed through the portal of the National Palace.

Such is the nervous nature of a nation that sometimes seems on the brink of chaos. In the past, Mexican militia often used excessive force in quelling demonstrations. The tactic today is to intimidate and overwhelm potential foes with numbers, rather than brute force.

There are stark reminders of the militarization of Mexico throughout the country, from the Guatemala border to Rio Bravo, from sand-bag bunkers in the countryside to squadrons in the city plazas. The army and the federal police are everywhere.

Thousands of soldiers have been enlisted to help fight the war on drugs. Mexican President Felipe Calderón in February committed 45,000 troops to halt the corruption and the slaughter perpetrated by rival drug cartels in nearly every corner of the nation, but especially on its northern frontier.

It's been a bloodbath on the border, where in the past year or so at least 7,000 people, including about 500 police, army and public officials, have been murdered. Sometimes the assassins are officers. The cartels' message of "get rich or get dead" has corrupted the entire police force in some communities, and their jobs have been taken over by soldiers and federal police.

While the extreme measure of firing the local cops and bringing in lots of militia has helped quell the violence in some areas, many Mexicans are uneasy with an armed camp controlling their communities. Thousands took to the streets in one embattled border city in early 2009 to protest the federal presence.

They remember the killings, the oppression, the abuses of power and of basic human rights that have been linked to the military over the past several decades. They're not fond of their corrupt cops, but they're not too comfortable with the military either.

They still recall the "Tlatelolco Massacre" when several hundred students were murdered by the military 10 days before the start of the Olympics in Mexico City. That happened in Oct. 2, 1968, but continuing investigations have made that date reverberate in the psyche of many Mexicans.

The university students had taken part in several peaceful political demonstrations when President Gustavo Diaz Ordaz ordered the army to occupy the National Autonomous University of Mexico, the nation's largest. It was the first time a Latin American country had hosted the Olympics and Diaz didn't want the rebellious students to upstage the event.

On Oct. 2, about 10,000 students gathered in the Plaza de Tres Culturas to protest the government action and they were soon surrounded by 5,000 soldiers, 200 tanks and trucks, with helicopters hovering over the plaza.

Before the night was over, perhaps as many as 300 were dead from gunshot wounds and thousands were injured and arrested. The Mexican government, facing one of its worst crises ever, launched a huge cover-up operation. It took 40 years for the truth to come out.

Among the facts revealed was that the United States had a role in the massacre. The CIA, fearing that the riots would disrupt the Olympic Games, had been monitoring the student actions each day. The U.S. then sent military radios, weapons and ammunition, along with riot control training materials to Mexico before and during the crisis.

It wasn't the first time the U.S. had intervened in the domestic affairs of a sovereign Latin American nation. And it wouldn't be the last.

A quarter century later, on Jan. 1, 1994, another insurrection sent a message across Mexico from its southernmost state, Chiapas. It was the day that the North American Free Trade Agreement went into effect.

Mexico's indigenous had been left out of the process. They had lost communal lands when the *ejidos* were sacrificed to prepare for NAFTA. Now they feared free trade would put an end to their way of life.

The Zapatista Army of National Liberation, or EZLN, a loosely formed coalition of Mayan Indians numbering about 3,000, took control of four Chiapas municipalities that New Year's Day. They were led by a charismatic masked man by the name of Subcomandante Marcos. They wanted to send a message to Mexico City.

The government wasn't interested in their message. It was having a peso crisis, and it didn't need an indigenous distraction on the birthday of NAFTA, which had been heralded to transform Mexico into a First World country.

Besides, it had gotten a message from Chase Manhattan Bank in New York "to get rid of the Zapatistas" in exchange for full bailout financing, promised by U.S. President Clinton.

The next day, thousands of troops were sent to Chiapas to crush the uprising, and over the course of the next 10 days, 145 people were dead and hundreds were arrested.

The conflict, however, went unresolved for years, with occasional flashpoints that ignited national interest in EZLN's demands. The Zapatistas had moved in on numerous idle ranches, land which had been promised to them by the revolutionary Emiliano Zapata back in 1911. The landowners, backed by paramilitary groups, attempted to oust them.

That set the stage for the "Acteal Massacre" of Dec. 22, 1997. State-trained and funded civil defense forces, armed with AK-47 assault weapons, surrounded a Catholic chapel in the Tsotsil Mayan community and opened fire. Forty-five Tsotsils were slain, including 15 children, 21 women and nine men.

Since that fateful New Year's Day in 1994, large areas of Mexico's majority indigenous states, especially Chiapas, Oaxaca and Guerrero, have come under virtual army control.

Mexico, unlike many Latin American nations, has been a bulwark of stability and civilian rule for more than 70 years. This is due to a balance of military and civilian power as dictated by the constitution. However, the army's role and its influence have grown in the past two decades.

In spite of the economic crisis of 1994-95, the government paid an estimated $2.2 billion to the U.S. for military purchases, a 40% increase over 1993 expenditures. An army general in 1996 took over the Mexico City police chief's post, and replaced nearly a hundred high command police assignments with army officers. Military officers have superceded civilian law enforcement leaders in 21 of Mexico's 31 states.

There's been a dramatic increase in the size and capacity of the Mexican Army Forces. Mexico increased its spending on the military from 2.6% of the government's total spending to 5.1% between 1985 and 1995. Two years later it had increased again by another 2.5%.

The total number of Mexicans in the armed forces doubled in the past two decades, now totaling about 250,000. The United States is Mexico's primary source of military aid, training and support. Since 1997, the U.S. has provided $112 million in military assistance in the form of training, arms and equipment.

Between 1996 and 1998, Mexico sent more military personnel to the U.S. for training than any country in the Western Hemisphere. In 1999, Mexico dipped to second place, behind Colombia.

The military has been called into several skirmishes with isolated guerrilla groups around the country over the past decade. Thousands of soldiers more recently have played a leading role in combating the drug wars and the violence and corruption caused by the cartels.

Most Mexicans are grateful that the army has stepped in to stop the bloodbath. What they're wary of is the military's track record of repression, of denying the time- honored tradition of free speech and peaceful protest.

The latest governmental incursion against civil rights took place on June 14, 2006, in downtown Oaxaca. An annual teachers' strike over pay, working conditions and support for poor students turned into a popular uprising when Oaxaca's governor ordered 1,000 state police into the historic central square to break up the teachers' protest camps. The attack took place at dawn, and included helicopters shooting tear gas.

The teachers regrouped in the *zócolo* and one month later they were joined by tens of thousands of sympathetic citizens. One solidarity march numbered 800,000 people. Besides the teachers' issues, the masses now demanded the governor's resignation.

It was the biggest social conflict in Oaxaca's history. Nearly six months of street clashes and military crackdowns resulted in the deaths of 23 people, including American journalist Brad Will, injuries to hundreds and arrests of 1,000 or more.

It also was the largest military buildup since the Zapatista uprising in 1994.

As the violence escalated, President Vincente Fox ordered 5,000 federal agents of the Federal Preventative Police to re-establish law and order. Two protesters were killed as the FPP forcefully took over the city square on Oct. 29.

Finally, in January 2007, the siege was over, the tourists returned to zócolo and an uneasy calmness descended over the city. But the root causes of the conflict have remained unresolved.

# Chapter Seven

## *Militarization – 2*

✦

### *U.S. antes up $1.6 billion for war on drugs*

On May 6, 2009, the 40-day blockade of the Trinidad mine in the Oaxaca community of San José del Progreso came to a sudden and violent halt as 700 federal police officers stormed into the community in anti-riot gear along with an arsenal of tear gas, dogs, assault rifles and a helicopter.

The authorities seemed geared to take on a heavily armed drug cartel, not a community protest. To many, the government's reaction also was an eerie reminder of Oaxaca's months-long social conflict in 2006.

The overwhelming show of force was in response to community residents' demand that the Canadian company Fortuna Silver Mines get out of town.

They didn't want "the foreigners to steal our natural wealth."

But they also were concerned about potential health hazards, with chemicals like cyanide and arsenic that are used in mining poisoning their water supplies. They were alarmed by the dynamite blasts that were shaking their community. They were worried about the future fertility of their lands and the impact that would have on their only livelihoods in agriculture and cattle.

They were upset that they weren't consulted about the plans for a mine that had the capacity of yielding 50 million ounces of silver worth about $700 million.

The Canadian company was in the exploration phase of developing the mine, but it had already invested $35 million in the project and it wasn't about to welcome an open dialogue with the neighbors.

So when the people started their peaceful protest, the Mexican army was called in to set up camp at the entrance to the mine.

It's all part of the legacy of the North American Free Trade Agreement. Communal lands, *ejidos*, were broken up and sold, and then direct foreign investment was given free reign in the country with government and military backing.

Mexico remains the top destination in Latin America for foreign investment. In a three-year period, multinational companies received more than 80 federal mining concessions, covering 1.5 million acres of land, just in the state of Oaxaca. Other mega-projects in the works include hydroelectric dam construction and oil exploration.

Nearly a decade earlier, Plan Puebla Panamá was unveiled to link the nine southern states of Mexico with Central America through a series of networked mega-projects. It was a multi-billion scheme to promote "regional integration" and development. It was integral to the Free Trade Area of the Americas (FTAA), a proposed extension of NAFTA. One project was the construction of more than 1,300 miles (2,100 kilometers) of power lines from Mexico to Panamá, estimated to cost $390 million. One goal was to sell electricity generated in the region to the U.S.

Plan Puebla Panamá was buffeted by criticism from the start. Its "neoliberal" model of development favored the interests of multinational corporations over local communities. The $50 billion plan was tabled as project after project was met with local opposition and was withdrawn.

Some of the projects, however, have been resurrected by individual governments, and may become part of "Plan Mesoamerica" in the next go-around.

Then in 2002 came the Bush National Security Doctrine. It was the most grandiose expression of U.S. hegemony since the Monroe Doctrine. The doctrine explicitly linked trade and security as two pillars of a vision positing that what was good for the U.S., was good for the world. The document dedicated a chapter to asserting a fundamental relationship between free markets and U.S. national security.

This led to the next step for NAFTA. It was something called "Security and Prosperity Partnership." It was launched in 2006 in secret after meetings of the "Three Amigos," Presidents George W. Bush and Vincente Fox and Prime Minister Paul Martin.

SPP has been dubbed "NAFTA-Plus," even though there has been no signed agreement between the U.S., Canada and Mexico. It's based on the principle that prosperity is dependent on security, and that all three countries share beliefs in freedom, economic opportunity and strong democratic institutions.

Beyond that lofty premise, however, are disturbing details.

The goals were to apply the Bush counter-terrorism model throughout North America under closer U.S. control and surveillance, and to protect investment and business throughout the region. SPP recognized North America as a "shared economic space" that needed to be protected.

U.S. Under-Secretary of State Thomas Shannon pointed out that with SPP, "To a certain extent, we're armoring NAFTA."

While NAFTA was signed before the terrorist attack of Sept. 11, 2001, SPP was born in the "War on Terrorism" era and reflects an inordinate emphasis on U.S. security.

It made the relationship between the U.S. trade and security agendas explicit, under the pretext of greater integration. Its accords mandated border actions, military and police training, modernization of equipment and adoption of new technologies, all under the logic of the U.S. counter-terrorism campaign.

It aimed to create a regional security plan based on pushing its borders out into a security perimeter that included Mexico and Canada.

Measures to coordinate security pressured Mexico to militarize its southern border and to adopt repressive measures toward Central and South Americans who presumably were in transit to the United States. The U.S. government in effect deputized the Mexican government and gave it millions of dollars worth of intelligence and military equipment to crack down on "human smuggling networks."

The Bush administration, through SPP provisions, wanted to create more advantageous conditions for transnational corporations and remove remaining barriers for the flow of capital and cross-border production. It also wanted to secure access to natural resources in the other two countries, notably oil.

"The prosperity of the United States relies heavily on a secure supply of imported energy," the document stated.

For U.S. oil companies and America's geopolitical interests, Mexico's nationalized petroleum sector and state-run company, PEMEX, has been a major obstacle. The Mexican government decides when and how much oil goes to the U.S. based on its own national needs.

The vast majority of Mexicans take pride in its nationalized oil industry. However, SPP documents seem to suggest a change of ownership. They cited the low productivity of PEMEX as a major regional problem, ordered studies of its poor performance and offered private investment as a cure.

Before the ink was dry on the Security and Prosperity Partnership documents, along came "Plan Mexico." That was the name chosen by critics because of its association with Plan Colombia, the United States' billion-dollar military aid and anti-drug package for that South American country that was running into heavy opposition.

"The Mérida Initiative" was named for the site of the accord reached by newly elected Mexican President Felipe Calderón and President Bush. It was labeled as a "regional security cooperation initiative." It turned into a $1.4 billion U.S. military aid package for Calderón's war on drugs.

The Mexican president, unlike his predecessors, got serious about combating drug trafficking and organized crime that had turned the northern frontier into a bloodbath.

In the fall of 2007, the U.S. Congress passed the Mérida Initiative with wide bi-partisan support, and by the end of 2008, more than $333 million was on its way to Mexico. The $1.4 billion package over a three-year period is a ten-fold increase in U.S. military aid to Mexico.

The first stage, which included an additional $65 million to Central America, provided Mexico's military and federal police with helicopters and surveillance aircraft to support interdiction and rapid response.

The eight Bell helicopters cost $13 million each and the two maritime patrol planes are listed at $50 million each, including training and maintenance.

Also in that package were funds for non-intrusive inspection equipment, ion scanners and canine units for Mexican customs along with secure communication systems to improve data collection.

The U.S. also set aside funds to train and strengthen the institutions of justice, the selection of a new police force and case management software to track investigations among other items.

Initially, 15% of the approved funds of $400 million were held back, pending a report by the State Department regarding four human rights requirements, a condition imposed by the U.S. Congress. That included an investigation and resolution to the Brad Will case, the U.S. journalist slain in Oaxaca during the 2006 social conflict.

The three-year aid package could amount to $1.6 billion when funds for Haiti, Dominican Republic and all Central American nations are included.

Much of the funding will never leave the U.S. It will go toward the purchase of U.S.-made helicopters, airplanes, surveillance software and goods and services provided by U.S. defense contractors. There are no direct transfers of money to the government of Mexico or to its private contractors.

According to U.S. State Department officials, 59% of the first phase funds were earmarked for civil agencies responsible for law enforcement and 41% for the operational costs for the Mexican Army and Mexican Navy.

Critics say the Mérida Initiative will prove to be just as ineffective as Plan Colombia has been in curbing that drug trade. They point out that the effort doesn't take into account the two major root causes of drug trafficking: U.S. demand and Mexico poverty.

No funds have been included for drug rehabilitation or to reduce drug demand in the U.S. It's the widespread drug use in the U.S. that makes drug trafficking profitable in Mexico, where 50 million people live in poverty.

Besides, the critics say, the U.S.-designed trade policies, such as NAFTA, generate unemployment and perpetuate poverty.

The initiative, they insist, restructures the U.S.-Mexico bi-national relationship, recasts economic and social problems as security issues, and militarizes Mexican society. They fear that the civil rights of Mexicans may be further sacrificed in the name of security, and that the U.S. training and equipment may be used to repress legitimate citizen protest.

They're already concerned that more than 800 complaints of human rights abuses had been filed against the military in the first half of 2008, double the rate of the year before.

They're uneasy about the military becoming too powerful in the face of state weakness, a chilling reminder of a more repressive era.

---

## Chapter Seven: MILITARIZATION: Among the sources cited:

Todd Miller, NACLA, "Megaprojects and militarization: A perfect storm in Mexico," May 19, 2009.

Witness for Peace publication, "Oaxaca conflict and social movement," 2009.

Global Exchange, San Francisco, CA, "Programs in the Americas," July 9, 2007.

Joe Cummings, Mexconnect, "Drugs, rebellion and Mexico's militarization," Jan. 1, 2006.

British Broadcasting Company, "Student riots threaten Mexican Olympics," Oct. 2, 1968.

Laura Carlsen, Americas Policy, "Deep Integration: The anti-democratic expansion of NAFTA," May 30, 2007.

U.S. Embassy, Mexico City, U.S.-Mexico at a Glance, "The Mérida Initiative," September 2008.

Laura Carlsen, Americas Program Special Report, "A Primer on Plan Mexico," May 5, 2008.

Chatino women cluster around a clay oven in the indigenous mountain village of Cieneguilla in the state of Oaxaca to make corn tortillas for the community.

# Chapter Eight

## *El Maiz – 1*

✦

### *NAFTA's exports include corn farmers*

Ernesto has been a farmer all his life. He's raised corn for food and for fodder. His father and grandfather both were farmers, on the same land not far from Guanajuato, Mexico. It's been in the family for generations. But now the land sits fallow.

Ernesto, 40, works on a huge dairy farm in Wisconsin. He's a valued employee. He sends most of his paycheck to his family in Mexico. His wife and five young children, along with his mother-in-law and a couple of cousins, live on his weekly earnings.

It's been that way for the past eight years. He wires money and regularly talks on the telephone. But he's never even seen his youngest son. His wife, Marta, was five-months pregnant when he left home.

The family lives in a tumbled-down hacienda that once was the pride of the region. A decade ago, the land was quite fertile. The 100-hectare parcel, in the past an *ejido* with twice that acreage, produced plenty of white corn for the tortilla market.

Ernesto and his big brother Pablo took over the farm when their father died suddenly of a heart attack. Pablo didn't take to farming like Ernesto did. He was single, a dreamer, who preferred city life. In 1993, when the Mexican government broke up the communal or *ejido* lands to give individual ownership to its users, he sold his half of the land and moved to Guanajuato and enrolled at the university.

Ernesto loved the land. He liked to take his oldest son, Miguel, then only five years old, aboard his tractor as he plowed and planted and harvested the crop in the field. Someday, he hoped, Miguel would take over the family farm.

There were good harvests and bad harvests, years with lots of rain and years of drought. But the corn crop usually paid the bills. Ernesto put in an irrigation system, drawing water from a nearby stream, to make sure he could weather a severe drought.

He had heard about something called NAFTA, and how Mexican corn farmers might someday be affected by the free trade agreement with the United States. He figured an irrigation system, although a major investment, might put him in good stead with whatever the future held in store. NAFTA went into effect in 1994, but certain agricultural crops, such as corn, would remain protected by tariffs until 2008.

Ernesto figured he had 10 years before NAFTA would mess with his life and his family farm.

But before the turn of the century, the writing was on the wall. Mexican farmers were leaving their fields in droves. Corn, produced by giant agribusinesses in Iowa, Nebraska and Kansas, was starting to flood the Mexican market.

Ernesto suddenly realized he wouldn't be able to compete with the U.S.-subsidized corporate farms, but he thought he still might find a niche for his product at the local tortilla plant.

It was the year 2000, and U.S.-imported corn was being used to make tortillas in Mexico. It was an uneven field. Agribusiness in America was highly efficient and heavily subsidized by the U.S. government. Mexican farmers were on their own, and so were the consumers of tortillas. There would be no subsidies, no price controls. It was no contest.

Ernesto's cornfields had survived two years of drought conditions, thanks to the irrigation ditches he carved through the land. But then one day the government shut off his water supply. He was drawing too much from the stream, and he was producing too little.

He was reminded that NAFTA was focused on exports, not on feeding the folks at home. A multi-national firm had purchased what was once his brother's half of the family farm and had plans to construct a massive tomato hothouse operation. It needed Ernesto's water source. After all, the tomatoes were bound for the U.S.

Ernesto prayed for rain, but it didn't come. He watched as the fledgling corn shoots wilted and turned to stubble. There would be no harvest, and no money for seeds and fertilizer for the next growing season.

He sat dejectedly in the shade of the shed, watching his dream wither and die. His son Miguel was at his side. Ernesto knew he was a good farmer, and a good father. But things now were out of his control. He had no idea how he would feed his family.

He had heard of some Mexican farmers who, forced off their farms by unfair trade, went to work for the competition in Kansas. Just the thought left a bitter taste in his mouth.

His father and his grandfather had worked the land ever since the 1920s. The family farm had supported their families quite well over the years. They weren't rich, but they weren't poor, either.

He talked it over with Marta. She had grown up on a farm, but her parents had died and her only brother sold the land and had gone to the United States. He was somewhere in Wisconsin, working on a mega-dairy farm.

Ernesto anguished over the decision to sell the family farm. He felt like that would be akin to betraying his heritage. Yet, he realized he didn't have much choice. He had to feed his growing family. Without access to irrigation, the corn crop would be doomed to failure. And even if rain fell on his fields, he'd never be able to sell his corn for a price that would turn a profit.

Family farms in Mexico, even those once profitable with as much as 125 acres, were a thing of the past, Ernesto sadly thought. He couldn't fight the system. He finally decided to offer his acreage to the U.S. agribusiness that was putting up a small village of plastic greenhouses to grow tomatoes for the U.S. market.

Ernesto had to swallow his pride. But he was going to get his price. He felt the company had deep pockets. He asked $1,000 an acre. That would bring in $125,000, enough to feed his extended family for quite awhile and perhaps send his children to college. The company countered with $100 an acre. Ernesto couldn't let his heritage slip away for such a paltry sum.

He thought the negotiations would continue and they'd settle with a compromise. But, no, that was the company's final offer. And Ernesto's, too.

Marta called her brother in Wisconsin that next evening. Yes, he said, there were lots of jobs available on the giant dairy farms. They paid up to $10 an hour. Some of the operations were entirely run by migrants, he said. And most of them were undocumented.

Ernesto had never been out of the state of Guanajuato, just a few hours north of Mexico City. But he knew lots of people who had gone to the U.S. for work. Many of them had been living in Wisconsin's Fox River Valley for at least a decade.

He wasn't interested in taking up residence there. He just wanted to stay a few years and send back money to his family. Perhaps, someday he could again grow corn on the family farm.

Ernesto hugged and kissed his wife, and wrapped all his children in a single embrace, except for Miguel who had climbed onto his shoulders. He boarded a bus in Guanajuato for Mexico City, and then another heading north to Ciudad Juárez, nearly a day away.

There he contacted a *"coyote"* to guide him across the Rio Bravo and through the staggered lines of the U.S. Border Patrol. As he climbed over the 12-foot chain link fence onto U.S. soil, he was immediately arrested. He was handcuffed and packed in a van with five others and transported across the bridge to Ciudad Juárez.

Two days later he again tried to cross. This time the *"coyote"* directed him through the desert toward the southeast corner of New Mexico. He got lost, ran out of water and, dehydrated and exhausted, he crawled onto a paved road – where he was again met by the Border Patrol.

This time he was shuttled to the El Paso Service Processing Center, a detention facility operated by the U.S. Immigration and Customs Enforcement agency. He was held behind bars for 10 days. Then he was returned to Ciudad Juárez, with a warning that another attempt to cross the border illegally would put him in prison for years.

Ernesto had no choice. He had to try again. His brother-in-law was waiting for him in Wisconsin. So was a job on a dairy farm. His family in Guanajuato was counting on him. And his money was running out.

He was approached by another *"coyote"* as he was pondering his next move while sitting on the steps of the cathedral in downtown Juárez. The smuggler made the sign of the cross as he sat beside Ernesto. For $2,000 he would guarantee that Ernesto would make it to Wisconsin this time.

Ernesto said he only had $500, but he could pay the rest within a couple of months once he got that job on the farm. He also offered to put up his land in Guanajuato as collateral.

It was an arduous journey, fording the river, climbing the fence, trekking through the desert, hiding by day and walking by night, ever vigilant to the presence of the Border Patrol. Ernesto and his group of five teenagers from Chiapas met a van that took them to Alamogordo, New Mexico. There they split up. Ernesto rode a series of buses heading north, and before the week was over he had arrived in Wisconsin.

It was early March, and winter wasn't ready to fold into spring. There was a foot of snow covering the cornfields, and the temperatures hovered about zero Fahrenheit. The cows were lined up in stanchions, emitting frosty vapors throughout the massive barn. Ernesto shivered, but he went to work. He was on the night shift, and 1,000 Holsteins needed to be milked.

It was a mega-farm south of Green Bay, with 1,000 acres and 1,000 producing cows, and a dozen Mexicans manning the operation around the clock. Once it was a collection of small family farms of 40 acres or so, where mom and pop and the kids  milked a few cows by hand early in the morning.

But family farms are a thing of the past in Wisconsin, too.

Ernesto moved in with his brother-in-law and four other Mexican workers in an old farmhouse abandoned when a family moved into the city. The job was hard and the conditions were harsh, but every week there was a paycheck that provided food for his family and hope for their future.

Ernesto faithfully called his wife every Friday evening. The telephone had been disconnected from their home when she couldn't pay the bill. Marta and the kids visit a friend's house each week to await her husband's call.

He has to wipe the tears from his eyes when Miguel, now a teenager, asks him when he's coming home. Ernesto always says soon. But he knows that's not true.

Someday, he hopes to have legal documents that will allow him to visit his family in Mexico. He doesn't want to travel by "*coyote*" ever again. Someday, he'd like to have his family visit Wisconsin – but certainly not the way he arrived eight years ago.

Someday, Ernesto would like to go home and grow corn and feed his family off the land once tilled by his grandfather.

# Chapter Eight

## *El Maíz –2*

✦

### *Rallying cry for corn: 'Sin maíz, no hay país'*

Ernesto is but one of an estimated two million Mexican farmers who have been forced off their lands and have emigrated to the United States since NAFTA set the rules in 1994.

Many of them have ended up working on huge U.S. farms that export their products to Mexico. In effect, they have to cross the border to grow food in the U.S. to feed their families in Mexico.

Mexico, an agrarian nation, has been devastated by the North American Free Trade Agreement. Unfair trade with the U.S. has been disastrous for the country's bean, chicken, pig and coffee farmers. Mexican agriculture has consistently been undersold by highly efficient, heavily subsidized U.S. imports.

But nothing has been hit harder than corn, and that resonates deeply within the Mexican soul. After all, it's where corn was born. It's indigenous to Mexico. It's tied to the identity of the country. *"Sin maíz, no hay país."* "Without corn, there's no country." That's the rallying cry of Mexicans who fear a U.S. takeover of their sacred grain.

For 10,000 years the inhabitants of Mexico have based their diets and their lives around corn. Pre-Columbian Indians worshipped a god of corn. Most Mexicans eat corn at every meal. Fifteen million Mexicans depend on corn for their livelihood.

But more and more, the corn on the Mexican market is coming from corporate farms in the U.S. Midwest.

Before NAFTA, Mexico controlled all its grain imports through restrictive licensing and high tariffs. Now both the U.S. and Canada enjoy preferential treatment for their grain exports to Mexico.

Before NAFTA, virtually all tortillas made in Mexico came from Mexican-grown corn. Today, that tradition is being threatened. White corn, the kind used in tortillas, had been cautiously guarded by the government. But in January 2008, the last protective tariff on corn was eliminated.

However, while NAFTA had permitted a 14-year phase-in before all corn could freely flow from the U.S. to Mexico, the food flood had already reached crisis levels. It was yellow corn, the kind used for feed in the rapidly expanding chicken and pork industries, that poured into Mexico. The quotas were mostly ignored.

Mexico soon became the second largest market for U.S. corn, buying virtually 100% of its imports from the United States, the biggest exporter of corn in the world.

Under NAFTA's phase-in program, the U.S. was permitted to export 2.5 million tons at the start, with a 3% increase each year. However, due to industrial demand, especially in the growing livestock and starch industries, Mexico has winked at those quotas, charging minimal duties on over-quota amounts. During that period, U.S. exports have regularly been nearly twice the tonnage allowed.

U.S. corn exports increased 240% in NAFTA's first decade. In 2003, more than 7.7 million metric tons were delivered. That was 3.8 million tons more than permitted in the agreement. About 15% of that total was white corn.

U.S. government subsidies to corporate corn farmers, to the tune of $10 billion a year, permitted the giant agribusinesses to sell their product for as much as $145 million below their costs.

Mexican farmers just couldn't compete. The country's total agricultural budget is about $1 billion.

The trade liberalization rules of NAFTA were based on the theory that farmers in the U.S., Canada and Mexico would compete on an "equal playing field." It isn't and they can't.

U.S. farmers collected an average governmental subsidy of $20,800 as part of the 2002 farm bill. The average Mexican farmer received $722 in annual subsidies, and that amount has declined in recent years. Small farmers, those with fewer than three hectares, were cut off from all governmental support in 2009.

Mexican and American corn farmers differ enormously in their efficiency and productivity. On the average, a U.S. corn producer farms 270 hectares (a hectare is 2.4 acres) and has a corn yield of 8.5 metric tons per hectare. An average Mexican corn producer has 10 hectares of land that yields 5.8 metric tons per hectare -- if the land is irrigated. If it's not, the yield is less than 2 tons. Only 10% of the farmers have access to irrigation, and only one-third of them use a tractor.

Soon after NAFTA went into effect, the market price for corn dropped by more than 70%. Cheap corn seemed like good news at least for Mexican consumers.

But then they were awakened by the stark reality that Mexico was no longer feeding its people. It was losing its food sovereignty. Forty per cent of its food was coming from abroad. It depended on the U.S. imports for one fifth of its corn, one third of its wheat, and 90% of its rice and soy.

Even though the price of corn had declined, the basic basket of food items had increased by 257% from 1994 to 2002.

Then they learned that as many as 400,000 Mexican farmers were leaving their lands every year. By 2003, more than 1.3 million small producers were forced off their farms. Many joined the swelling ranks of Mexico's urban unemployed. Others migrated to the U.S. to pick crops. Former farmers became day laborers.

Oxfam International in a report issued in 2003 claimed there was a direct link between agricultural policies in the U.S. and rural misery in Mexico. The $10 billion subsidy paid to U.S farmers has led to cheap American corn flooding the Mexican market, destroying the livelihoods of Mexican corn farmers.

Carnegie Endowment in a similar report the same year noted that small farmers were coerced into selling their land to large operations that produce for export. They degrade the environment by using more water and chemical fertilizers to remain competitive.

Corn as animal fodder, rather than food for humans, is relatively new to Mexico. However, thanks to NAFTA and cheap yellow corn from the U.S., factory farming has created feedlots and pollution problems, as well as a drastic change in the Mexican diet.

The U.S. also is exporting large volumes of corn products, such as high fructose corn syrup, that impacts Mexico's sugar industry. Sugar was on NAFTA's phase-in list. Mexico's 20% tax on the syrup, adopted in 2002 to protect its sugar industry, was lifted in 2006. That opened the way for the U.S. to export 250,000 tons that year, and 500,000 tons in 2007. Agribusiness giant Archer Daniels Midland expected its export volume to increase even more in the future with the lifting of all tariffs in January 2008.

Now as American corn continues to flood the Mexican market, and more and more Mexican farmers have been forced out of business, the price of the grain has taken an upward spiral.

The deregulated price of the tortilla soared by 127% between 1997 and 1999, and jumped another 22% between 2000 and 2002.

In the summer of 2006, tortilla prices again skyrocketed. Food riots erupted throughout the country over the rising price of white corn, most of which was produced on small Mexican farms. There are 45,000 tortilla producers and 10,000 millers, but 90% of corn flour production is concentrated in two of Mexico's largest food companies, Gruma and Grupo Minsa.

Then there came ethanol, and its $3 billion taxpayer subsidy aimed to help curb the United States' dependence on foreign oil. Cornfields were taken out of the food business to make fuel for cars and trucks. Some 27 million tons of corn were dedicated to the production of ethanol between 2006 and 2007.

And with demand trumping supply, corn prices again took a spike throughout Mexico.

More than 100,000 took to the streets of Mexico City in 2007 to protest the approaching end of the corn tariffs, saying that would put Mexican corn out of business.

The International Food Policy Research Institute in 2008 projected a 66% increase in the price of corn over the next decade, attributed to biofuel production. In its report that said the world was eating more food than it was producing, the institute warned that biofuel production runs the risk of creating social unrest.

Adding insult to injury, the U.S. introduced genetically modified corn back in 1996 and within five years it had become 30% of the national harvest. The Mexican government feared that the corn seed entering the country with the imports could contaminate its stock, and it imposed a moratorium on planting transgenic crops. However, the measure was never enforced, and corn imports continued with no controls.

In 2001 it was discovered that peasants had unknowingly planted the seeds in their fields. It now threatens Mexico's genetic biodiversity, a product of 10,000 years of evolution.

Small farmers who grow corn in southern Mexico are responsible for maintaining the genetic diversity of the species. While American farmers raise a small handful of genetically nearly identical hybrids, Mexico's small farmers grow hundreds of different, open-pollinated varieties, commonly called landraces. Such diversity comes in handy, such as in 1970 when a fungus decimated the American corn crop and genes for resistance were found in a landrace in southern Mexico.

The cheap U.S. corn that is evicting those farmers from their land threatens to dry up the pool of genetic diversity upon which the future of the species depends.

Or as one indigenous leader in Oaxaca said, "The pyramids could be destroyed, but a fistful of corn is the legacy that we can pass on to our children and grandchildren."

---

## Chapter Eight: EL MAIZ: Among the sources cited

Debbie Seidband, AgExporter, "U.S. corn exports to Mexico thrive under NAFTA," January 2004.

Michael Pollan, Los Angeles Times, "A flood of U.S. corn rips at Mexico," April 23, 2004.

Elizabeth Becker, The New York Times, "U.S. corn subsidies said to damage Mexico," Aug. 27, 2003.

Stephen Zahniser, Amber Waves, "Mexico's corn industries and U.S.-Mexico corn trade," June 2004.

USDA, Economic Research Service Report, "U.S.-Mexico corn trade during NAFTA," 2004.

Lorraine Heller, Food Navigator, "ADM to increase corn syrup exports to Mexico," Sept. 7, 2006.

Jim Lane, Ethanol Promotion Council, "U.S. corn exports rose 6 per cent in 2007," March 27, 2008.

Ken Bensinger, The Washington Times, "Mexican corn comes a cropper," Sept. 9, 2003.

Carmelo Ruiz Marrero, Interhemispheric Resource Center, "Biodiversity in danger," June 2004.

Nikhil Aziz, Grassroots International, "NAFTA is killing tradition of corn in Mexico," Nov. 9, 2007.

Silvia Chavela Rivas, Noticias de Oaxaca, "Excluyen de apoyos a 450,000 productores de maiz," Feb. 24, 2009.

Leaders of the Chatino community in Cieneguilla, Oaxaca, gather on the basketball court in front of the municipal building to greet a contingent of visitors from North Carolina.

# Chapter Nine

## *OAXACA to NC – 1*

♦

### *Chatinos work in NC tobacco fields*

There's a white 2001 Chrysler Caravan, with North Carolina license plates, parked on a muddy slope in the mountaintop village of Cieneguilla in Oaxaca, Mexico.

It's a bit beat up, but it's the best-looking van in the community. It's the only one.

Roberto uses it to get to work – nearly 3,000 miles away in Durham, N.C.

He's home in the tiny Chatino village where he was born, and where all his kinfolk and friends reside, when they're not in North Carolina. In a few months, he's scheduled to go back to Durham and work in the tobacco fields.

He's been going back and forth to live and make a living for nearly a decade. Along the way he got his papers, and a Green Card, and a driver's license, and finally he bought a van. It was an easier commute.

Besides, there was room for at least eight other migrants who'd help pay for the gas. He'd drive them to the Ciudad Juárez where they'd contact a *coyote* to guide them across the border, and then he'd pick them up again in Texas, at a designated spot 30 miles north. Some of his passengers were regulars, undocumented, but experienced travelers.

Most indigenous migrants from Oaxaca still gravitate to California and the Northwest to work in the fields. But lately many have spread out to work in agriculture in other parts of the U.S.

Roberto was among a pioneer group of Chatinos, one of 16 indigenous communities in the state of Oaxaca, who were recruited to work on the East

Coast about 10 years ago. The word had gotten out, and North Carolina became one of the fastest growing Latino populations in the country.

The 1990 census counted 76,726 Hispanics in North Carolina. By the year 2000, the number had soared to 378,963 and just two years later it was estimated at more than 500,000. While there were Puerto Ricans and Cubans, along with other Central and South Americans in the state, two out of three Latinos came from Mexico.

The Latino population in North Carolina is quite diverse, with many regions in Mexico represented. The indigenous migrants, however, generally stick to their own communities. They're more comfortable with their customs and their distinct languages. Most speak Spanish as a second language.

They're mostly male, 60%, and they're young, with a median age of 24.

In the past, the Latinos in North Carolina were migrant workers who arrived and left with the "picking seasons." While many are still employed in agriculture, their seasons have been extended year-around. North Carolina is the fifth most populous farm-worker state in the U.S., with an estimated 200,000 workers, the majority Hispanic. It ranks behind California, Texas, Washington and Florida.

Latinos drive the state economy. North Carolina's tobacco, greenhouse and nursery, vegetable and fruit industries rely heavily on the labor of farm workers to produce more than $2.2 billion in sales.

Migrants aren't just farm workers these days. Almost one in four is working in construction and maintenance and a large number have landed jobs in production and transportation, and still others are in service industries, including restaurants.

Roberto, and his fellow Chatinos, landed jobs in the tobacco fields back in the late 1990s. The Tarheel State still was the nation's No. 1 producer of tobacco, a tradition that traces its history all the way back to Sir Walter Raleigh in 1586.

In 2007, tobacco employed 255,000 workers in North Carolina and had 166,000 acres in production, generating income of $587 million and had a total economic impact of $7 billion.

The Durham area became the focal point of Mexican migration.. Chatino community members, however, have spread out to Raleigh, Greensboro and Winston-Salem, all along Interstate 40.

After three years of working in the tobacco industry, Roberto returned to Cieneguilla, hoping to find a job that could keep him at home. Farming was no longer an option in his village. NAFTA had seen to that. His ancestors had made a good living growing coffee beans, but that industry had collapsed due to worldwide competition, a market glut and record low prices.

Up to the turn of the century, relatively few people from Cieneguilla, especially those involved in coffee production, had migrated north. Mexico was the No. 6 producer/exporter of coffee in the world. From harvest to brew, the industry employed     three million people. Two-thirds of the producers were indigenous small landholders.

But then, beginning in 2001, an unprecedented amount of low quality coffee from Vietnam inundated the world market, depressing prices to historic lows. The glut was the result of a debt rescue plan put out by the International Monetary Fund and the World Bank. Their agro-export policy to earn revenue to pay off foreign loans greatly increased the supply of coffee and resulted, within five years, in Vietnam becoming the world's second largest coffee exporter.

As supply exceeded demand, coffee prices dropped and severely impacted Mexico's indigenous coffee producers. The costs of production exceeded their income, some took out loans at high interest rates to temporarily make ends meet, and as a result, they accrued debts that locked them into poverty.

Thus, with coffee a losing proposition and agriculture extremely limited by both topography and subsidized, cheap imports from the U.S., the migration to the north gained momentum. Other indigenous villages in state of Oaxaca had long sent workers to the U.S. In fact, many thrived on the remittances sent back by their members.

It was Cieneguilla's turn to test the U.S. job market.

The remote village, perched atop a heavily pine-forested ridge, is one of a number of isolated Chatino-speaking settlements scattered about the Sierra Madre del Sur mountain range.

Cieneguilla doesn't get many visitors. It's a two-hour drive from Juquila, up an eroded, muddy mountain road which winds and dips through stands of towering pines. Four-wheel-drive vehicles are needed to ford numerous creek beds.

On most days there are a lot of visitors at the base of the mountain. It's a place of pilgrimage to the Virgin of Juquila, which draws thousands of pilgrims who regularly process along Highway 131 from El Pedimento to Santa Catarina Juquila.

It's an 18th century shrine that houses a tiny image of the virgin, believed to be miraculous, which traces its beginnings back to 1633. The feast of the Virgin of the Conception, which draws people from throughout the state of Oaxaca and beyond, is celebrated on Dec. 8 with a huge fair, fireworks and indigenous dances.

Cieneguilla and Juquila are connected by a lone pickup truck stationed on the mountain that transports villagers to town for festivities, for shopping and for schooling.

The older generation in Cieneguilla speak only Chatino, one of 16 distinct indigenous languages spoken in the state. The others speak Spanish, but only as a second language.

Chatinos, according to the 2005 census, number 42,477, which puts them in sixth place. The major groups of Zapotec and Mixtec together total about 650,000 people. The other 14 combined amount to 500,000. More than one-third of the state's population of 3.5 million is indigenous.

While the numbers are large, the settlements are quite small. Cieneguilla, at last count, had a population of just 551. And that included the 136 members who were living in North Carolina in 2009.

There's a list of those who had gone to the U.S. on the wall of the municipal building. Next to their names is the amount of money they've sent back to the community. There are large trees planted and protected around the village square, the basketball court and the Catholic church. Each was donated by a U.S. worker. Modest but new houses, made of lumber, and even a few of brick, dot the village, visible signs of family remittances.

Many homes in the village have running water, electricity, telephones and television sets. Outhouses still prevail, however, as do cold shower stalls in the backyards. Clay-mounded, wood-fed ovens in separate huts are still preferred to modern kitchen appliances.

Life is better now in Cieneguilla, most would agree, thanks to the money being sent back from the U.S. Before 1995, most of the houses were built with adobe and thatch. The remittances have spurred a construction and remodeling boom, along with other cottage industries.

Roberto has witnessed the vast changes in his native village over the past decade. He returns home every couple of years, and is always amazed at the transformation that has taken place in Cieneguilla. His savings have built new houses for his parents, as well as for his wife and three children. A basic dwelling can be built for $1,200, easily accessible out of a year's pay in the U.S.

But he recognizes that while his money has provided a more comfortable life for his family, his prolonged absence from their lives has taken its toll. He feels less connected to the community, too.

This time Roberto decided to stick around Cieneguilla for awhile. Community service, or *cargo*, had been taken over by women, due to so many men being away. So he volunteered to be the sexton at the church. Then to cap off his new title as *mayordomo*, he sponsored a fiesta for the community, with *barbacoa* and beverages for all.

Roberto realizes that the money will run out someday soon, and he'll have to return to North Carolina to replenish his supply. He also worries that if the U.S. economy continues to worsen, there might be fewer jobs there for the people of Cieneguilla.

Yet, that might not be so bad, he says, if only there were work is the town of his birth.

# Chapter Nine

## *Oaxaca To NC – 2*

✦

### *One-third of indigenous live in U.S.*

Tourists from all over the world flock to Oaxaca to savor the cuisine, the archeological treasures, the pine and oak forests, the rugged mountains and the friendly seashore coves as well as the customs and costumes of so many indigenous people.

The state of Oaxaca has everything – except jobs.

Thousands, forced off their lands by trade policies, flee every day for the north and beyond the border in search of a better life. The one their ancestors enjoyed for generations now is gone.

Oaxaca is Mexico's second poorest state, next to Chiapas, its neighbor to the east. The United Nations ranks Oaxaca second to last in Mexico on the human development indicators of life expectancy, education and income.

More than one-third of its citizens are indigenous. They speak 16 different languages, and most cannot understand the villagers on the next mountain top. About 40% speak only their native tongue. There are more speakers of indigenous languages than in any other state in Mexico.

The rugged terrain, which caused communities to develop in relative isolation from one another, is responsible for the cultural and linguistic diversity of the region.

The Zapotec and the Mixtec have dominated indigenous Oaxaca for centuries, long before the Conquistadores. The Zapotec commanded the central Valley of Oaxaca, one of the most fertile areas in the Americas, until they were conquered by the Mixtec in the 13th century. There they harvested a wide variety of domesticated plants and fruits, from tomatoes to peppers, and from avocados to pineapples.

Then came the Spanish and Hernán Cortés. He was granted Oaxaca as his prize for conquering New Spain for the Spanish crown. The conquerors cultivated wheat and sugar cane in the fertile valley, and enslaved the natives, forcing them to work in the gold and silver mines. Disease and harsh treatment decimated the indigenous.

Many did escape, however, by retreating into the remote, mountainous regions. There they have lived for centuries, farming difficult terrain. It wasn't fertile like the central valley, but the sparse land was just right for *milpas,* the traditional practice of planting corn, beans, lima beans and squash in the same plot.

Most now grow corn and beans on small farms in the valleys, and some grow coffee on the hillsides, but that too is fading, another victim of trade policies. More than half of all Oaxacans made their living by farming, most of it on communally held lands. But just before NAFTA was enacted, the *ejidos,* peasant land reform won through revolution, were scrapped by a stroke of President Carlos Salinas' pen.

Other than the central Valley of Oaxaca, it's hard to find much flat land in a state that claims two mountain ranges, Sierra Madre Oriental and Sierra Madre del Sur. The state is the fifth largest in size, with nearly 37,000 square miles. The average altitude is a mile high. And the area is subject to occasional earthquakes, the latest one being a 6.4 magnitude *temblor* recorded Feb. 12, 2008.

The official name of the capital city is Oaxaca de Juárez, named for Benito Juárez, Mexico's only indigenous president. He grew up in a Zapotec village, worked on the land and as a domestic servant before entering a seminary. Later he became a lawyer and a judge. He served two terms as president between 1861 and 1872.

Monte Albán, the capital of the ancient Mixtec-Zapotec empire, today is the region's major archeological destination, although Mitla, "the place of the dead" in Zapotec, is also a tourist draw, especially for its unique tile work and patterns that are reflected in arts and crafts throughout Mexico.

The Mixtec and Zapotec people today account for more than 650,000 of a total state population of 3.5 million. Fourteen other registered indigenous communities, from the Mazateco with 165,000 to the Popoloco with just 61 people, make up the remaining 500,000 indigenous.

Oaxaca, traditionally an agriculture state with little industry, over the years has sent thousands of its young people north to find work. But most of them have stayed within Mexico, finding jobs in the northwest states of Sonora, Sinaloa and Baja California. When the *Bracero* "guest worker" program was open from 1942 to 1964, many headed for the U.S.

Mexico's economic crisis of 1982, however, opened the floodgates. Tens of thousands crossed the border to find work in the agricultural fields of

California. By 1990 there were more than 110,000 Zapotec and Mixtec migrants living in the Los Angeles area and in California's central valley.

Then came NAFTA and the Peso Crisis of 1994, and the migration surge continued. It's estimated that there are 1.5 million migrants from Oaxaca now living in the U.S. That's more than one-third of those born in the state. Even more Oaxacans have migrated to northwest Mexico. The state is now ranked second in the country for sending migrants.

For years, Oaxaca's small scale producers depended on subsidies and services to make ends meet. Most of the farmers worked on communal lands. The withdrawal of government support from the agricultural segment, and the demise of the *ejido* system, combined with falling market prices for basic grains, brought on by a flood of cheap, subsidized food from the U.S., have produced a major crisis for Oaxaca farmers.

It also has accelerated the migration movement to the north.

An estimated 200,000 Oaxacans now migrate to the U.S. each year. Most are young men. Rare is the household in Oaxaca that doesn't have at least one member living in the U.S. Sixty per cent of indigenous migrants from Oaxaca are under 19 years old. On the average they've had a total of six years of schooling. Most speak Spanish, as a second language, but many are more comfortable speaking the tongue of their community.

But while other Mexican migrants have somewhat reluctantly adopted the U.S. as their new home -- even if they don't have legal papers -- Oaxaca's indigenous see their time away from their community as a temporary necessity. They maintain strong ties with their ethnic community, both in the U.S. and back in Oaxaca. Most remain a total of six years or less, broken up by home stays, and then return to contribute to their community.

California continues to be the top drawing card for Oaxaca migrants, although clusters of ethnic groups have spread out to other agricultural states, like Oregon and Washington, Florida and Arizona. When Oaxacans migrate, they go wherever their kinfolk are.

The Trique community, which numbers only 18,000 in Oaxaca, are influential in Oregon's farm workers union. Florida's Coalition of Immokalee Workers speak Oaxacan dialects. The Zapotec community is especially strong in the Los Angeles area.

One tiny village in the mountains of Oaxaca has had a presence in Los Angeles for almost 30 years. Migrants come and go, almost on a rotating basis. But while they're in California working in the fields, they're also building their community back home.

Soledad Teitilian is not on most Mexican maps. But the village has become renowned in Los Angeles for its benefit basketball tournaments.

Oaxacan natives tend to be short, and no one aspires to play for the Lakers. But basketball, not soccer, is their game.

That's due to the rugged, mountainous terrain of their homeland. There are few wide-open spaces that are needed for soccer or baseball. Basketball hoops and courts are prevalent in most villages, especially in front of municipal buildings.

So the natives of that tiny village put on a basketball tourney in the Pico-Union district of Los Angeles that drew 50 teams and raised money – 3 million pesos was the goal – to repair the adobe church in their community back home.

It wasn't the first time the Oaxacan migrants got together to raise funds for their village. Over the past 10 years, they have helped secure potable drinking water, they have built a municipal building and a chapel for the old church, and they've put a roof over the municipal basketball court.

While Oaxacan ethnic communities are dispersed throughout the agricultural areas of the U.S., they have found a way to unite, not just around their language and their towns of origin, but also around their traditions and their identity as indigenous migrants.

At first it was an effort to unite three Mixtec and two Zapotec migrant associations in California. But then other language groups were added to form the Binational Oaxacan Indigenous Front to promote community and workplace struggles for social justice.

It's a much needed cause.

Oaxaca's indigenous are seen as the most vulnerable of migrant workers. Some are illiterate, others can't speak Spanish. They know little about the modern world, its culture or its economy.

Agribusinesses in northwest Mexico, along with their counterparts in the U.S. and especially California, openly recruit in Oaxaca, preferring the indigenous worker to the mestizo, the established migrant worker.

Employers say they work harder, and they put up with lower wages and bad working conditions. They say their short stature is ideal for harvesting fruits and vegetables. They say "Oaxacans like to work bent over."

Many have been abused and have been stung by racist remarks. Fellow Mexicans, mestizos in supervisory positions, label them Indians as an insult, meaning dirty, stupid and backward. The same prejudice that they experienced in Mexico is repeated in the fields of California.

Few ever progress from being field hands. They lament that being Oaxacan qualifies them to work in the fields and nothing more.

They're also more likely to be ripped off by unscrupulous employers who cheat them out of overtime pay, or promised benefits, or even with fake checks.

Still, they come to California and an increasing number of agricultural states. They have no choice. In Oaxaca, there are virtually no jobs besides subsistence farming.

At least in the United States, there's a payday that promises a reward 10 times as much as they might have made – if they could have gotten get a job.

They realize it's all temporary. After a few years, they'll be back in their villages with their families. Perhaps they'll be able to build a new house, or at least fix up the old one. Maybe an indoor bathroom with a shower. Maybe they'll get involved in community service, or perform *tequio,* a voluntary task, like policing or maintenance, jobs that have become women's roles in the absence of so many men.

After several years in the U.S., Oaxacan migrants will likely see a big difference in the communities they left behind. There'll be new buildings, streets, playgrounds and schools, thanks to their remittances.

Oaxacans are generous toward their indigenous communities. On the average, Mexicans send back 10% of what they earn in the U.S. In 2003, Oaxacans gave a total of $647 million to families and villages. The state ranked fifth in remittances, even though Oaxacans weren't among the top states represented in the U.S.

Their remittances averaged $365 each month, more than double that of the going wage in Oaxaca. A large chunk of that money went for home construction and renovation as well as helping out with daily living costs like food and utilities.

The migrants' money has made living a bit easier back home, but that has come at a cost. Couples are split up for years at a time, leading to a disintegration of family life, a shifting of traditional male-female roles in the community and that has increased the incidence of psychological problems, stress and anxiety, which in turn impact physical well-being.

In recent years, Oaxacans have gotten used to living away from home. But if they had their druthers, the indigenous would much rather stay put in their tranquil, hillside communities.

---

## Chapter Nine: OAXACA to NC: Among the sources cited:

Jeffrey H. Cohen, Pennsylvania State University, "The Oaxaca-U.S. connection," January 2005.

Witness for Peace Publication, Oaxaca, Mexico, "Crisis in the countryside," January 2009

Mireya Oliverea, LA Beez, "Basketball much more than sport for Oaxacans in Los Angeles," March 14, 2009.

David Bacon, America's Program, "Binational Oaxacan indigenous organizers face new century," Aug. 21, 2002.

Brett Wilkison, UC Berkeley Graduate School of Journalism, "An unspoken class system," March 2006.

Andrew Leonard, How the World Works, "Oaxacans like to work bent over," May 14, 2007.

Regina Cortina, Learn NC,  University of North Carolina, "From rural Mexico to North Carolina," January 2006.

Franco Ordonez, Moorsville Tribune, "Flow of illegal immigrants into NC drying up," April 15, 2009.

Jordan Green, Yes! Weekly, "Border Crossings," March 18, 2009.

A cross is planted near the crossroads of the migrant trail in Sonora in remembrance of the thousands of Mexicans who died in the desert trying to reach the U.S. for a better life.

# Chapter Ten

## Guanajuato To WI – 1

✦

### La Cañada's exodus is Bracero tradition

Hector León was just following the family tradition. When he got to be 16, it was time for him to go to the United States and work in the fields.

His grandfather did it. So did his father and his brother and uncles and lots of cousins. They all left La Cañada, a small village in the central Mexican state of Guanajuato, and followed the lettuce harvest from Florida to Wisconsin.

It all started with the *Bracero* program in which the U.S. recruited millions of Mexicans to harvest the crops during the World War II labor shortages. The migrant workers were welcomed into the U.S. for more than two decades until the program ended in 1964.

By then it had become a tradition, a way of life for the men of Guanajuato, and especially La Cañada. And since they now couldn't get legal documents, they came by *coyote*. At first the men worked the harvest and then returned home. But as it became more difficult to cross the border, they moved from farms to cities, found year-around jobs and brought their families to the U.S.

Hector León remembers his first trip to the U.S. He was with his father, brother and cousin and they were all packed in the trunk of a *coyote's* clunker car. They had paid $300 apiece to get from Tijuana to Los Angeles. It was a journey that he swore he would never do again.

It was 1982, and his father, Salvador, and the others had to get back to Wisconsin to tend to their plot of tomatoes and green peppers near the town of Red Granite. They had rented acreage to start their own business and put down roots in central Wisconsin.

The previous September, while celebrating Mexico's independence day in Montello, they had been rounded up by immigration officials and deported.

They had land in the U.S., albeit rental property. They continued to follow the lettuce harvest from Florida to the north but they had a stake in Wisconsin. Uncle Fermín married a Latina from Texas, a U.S. citizen, and they took up residence in Neenah, Wisconsin, for awhile. He later moved to California and became a highly successful horse breeder and trainer.

Hector worked in the fields for awhile, but he soon moved to Appleton, enrolled at Fox Valley Technical College, learned English, got his G.E.D. high school diploma and studied accounting. Later he earned a bachelor's degree in accounting from Lakeland College and landed a good job with Schroeder Moving Systems.

Hector, still a teenager, became the "pioneer" settler and contact person for families from La Cañada in Wisconsin's Fox River Valley. In 1986, he applied for and received legal residency via the amnesty program. At that time, there were but a half-dozen Mexicans from La Cañada living in northeastern Wisconsin. Two decades later, that number had grown to thousands. Today there are many more living in Wisconsin than in La Cañada.

Not long after Hector León and his kinfolk settled down in the Fox Valley, another large prominent family from La Cañada came to Wisconsin. Martín Vargas, the middle child of Luis and Benita Vargas, was just 21 when he arrived in the U.S. He stayed with Hector León at first, and his sister later married one of Hector's cousins.

Over the years, all but one of Martín's siblings came to live in the Fox Valley. Luis and Benita had 16 children and now count 48 grandchildren. Martin estimates that there are more than 350 Vargas relatives now living in the Appleton area. Six of his brothers run their own businesses in construction and maintenance.

La Cañada de Caracheo once claimed a population of about 10,000 people. Today there are fewer than 2,000, mostly older people. There's a brand new church and lots of new houses, thanks to remittances and the generosity of the native sons and daughters living in the U.S. But the buildings are empty for most of the year, and so are the shops and the streets.

The village was founded in 1612. It straddles a plain about a mile high between two hills, from which it gets its Spanish name, in the municipality of Cortazar. The second part of its name, Caracheo, means "dried water" in the Tarascan language. And that tells the tale of the exodus.

It's an agricultural area -- when it rains. Some years it doesn't, and without irrigation, the crops wither. There have been long periods of drought in recent years, and that has coaxed thousands to leave the region in search of work – mostly in the U.S.

Hector worked in the auto industry in nearby Celaya for awhile, but in the back of his mind was the siren call of America. Every male in his extended family had made his living off the land, not in Guanajuato but in the United States. He was the second oldest of five children, and his big brother had already been to the U.S., and it was now his turn.

Hector was a year short of graduation from high school when he left. Most of his peers dropped out of school before sixth grade to work in the fields. But he had other goals. He was going to go to the U.S. to live. He wasn't going to commute back and forth each year. He was going to learn English, finish high school and go on to college and find a good job, away from the lettuce fields of his father and his uncles.

Hector is now 43, a college-educated accountant who lives with his wife Marisa and two sons, Osvaldo, age 11, and Octavio, 7, in an upscale neighborhood in suburban Appleton. He and his wife are involved in the Cub Scouts and Boy Scouts. He became a U.S. citizen in 1996.

He hasn't forgotten his roots, however. His family vacations in Mexico, and quite often he hosts fiestas and barbeques at his expansive house for friends and relatives from La Cañada.

Each year during the second week of March, the village exodus is reversed. Thousands flock to La Cañada, from Wisconsin, from California, from wherever they live in the U.S. to pay homage to their hometown saint – and to party. The annual reunion is a must for most, even for those without documents who risk the return to the U.S.

The village bustles with activities for several weeks and then becomes a ghost town once again. It's been that way for decades.

It was 80 years ago when Padre Elias Nieves became a martyr of the Catholic Church. He was a simple parish priest who tended to his flock in La Cañada during tumultuous times when the Mexican government intensified its persecution of the church.

He was just 44 when a federalist firing squad cut short his ministry on March 10, 1928. He was beatified by Pope John Paul II in July 1997.

Padre Nieves was a bit frail and somewhat timid, not a wild-eyed revolutionary as the times seemed to foster. His strength came from the people to whom he ministered. He was faithful to them and they to him, and today tens of thousands of their descendants call him blessed.

Jesús Sierra and his brother Dolores were gunned down while trying to protect the priest from the Mexican militia. Both the León and Vargas families claim kinship with the two brothers.

The government's assault on the church created defenders among the faithful, especially in La Cañada and throughout rural Guanajuato. They took up arms and formed rag-tag units to challenge the Mexican troops. They were called "*Cristeros*," followers of Christ.

The Cristeros were particularly strong in the state of Guanajuato, and in communities like La Cañada. When Padre Nieves was ordered by the government to leave his parish in 1926 and face house arrest in Mexico City, his parishioners rallied to his side.

They hid him in a cave near the hill of La Gavia, where he offered daily mass and continued to administer the sacraments for the next 14 months. But one day as he left the cave he encountered a posse of soldiers. They noticed mass vestments beneath his white peasant's cloak. He was forced to admit he was a priest, and he was arrested along with two companions, the Sierra brothers.

His parishioners pleaded for his release, and even offered ransom money. But the priest said no. At dawn on March 10, 1928, the soldiers marched Padre Nieves and the Sierra brothers to a plaza in nearby Cortazar. There they died before a firing squad.

Padre Nieves gave his watch to the captain and blessed the soldiers who were kneeling before him. His final words were "Viva Cristo Rey!" Long live Christ the King.

There were a number of battlefields in the countryside of Guanajuato, and there were other priests who died before firing squads during the Cristero revolt. A number of communities can claim their own martyr, and many continue to commemorate them long after their deaths.

Each year on Jan. 5, the day before Epiphany, thousands climb Cublete Mountain not far from the city of Guanajuato to pray before the 65-foot statue of Christ the King. Most make the three-day pilgrimage on horseback. It's called a "*cabalgata*" and the faithful, descendants of Cristeros, come from Chicago and Texas, as well as other parts of Mexico to remember their heritage and underscore their devotion to *Cristo Rey*.

Each year on March 10, a shorter version of the *cabalgata* takes place in La Cañada. Thousands make the pilgrimage on foot and on horseback from the village square to Cortazar, about six miles away, the route Padre Nieves and the Sierra brothers were forced to march to their deaths.

Many of the pilgrims are from the northeastern Wisconsin. The Vargas and León families rarely miss the opportunity to return to the village to pay homage to their hometown saint and to get together with friends and relatives scattered across America.

Most stick around a couple of weeks to attend fiestas and celebrations in honor of Nuestra Señora de los Dolores, the name of the church that Padre Nieves served for just seven years. And then they return home and La Cañada once again is at rest for another year.

Meanwhile, back in Wisconsin and elsewhere where the villagers have settled, the stories of Padre Nieves and the Cristeros resound from the pews of Catholic churches and banquet halls for those who couldn't make it to Mexico.

More than 1,000 regularly attend a special mass at Santa Teresita Church in Appleton on March 10, the feast day of their favorite saint. They then participate in a pageant and a celebration that takes them back to the place and to the people they left behind.

# Chapter Ten

## *Guanajuato To WI – 2*

✦

### *Immigrants send money to 'ghost towns'*

Its motto is "*La Tierra de Oportunidades.*" The land of opportunity.

The Mexican state of Guanajuato boasts fertile agricultural fields, rich silver mines, dramatic mountains and valleys, a developed drawing card for tourism and a prodigious past that puts it at the top of the class.

Long before the Spanish arrived, the native Tarascan Indians named their land "Guanajuato." In their language it means "the place of frogs." They believed frogs represented the God of Wisdom.

Some question whether that wisdom has been passed down today as they mull its questionable future.

More than one-third of those who were born in the state of Guanajuato are now living and working in the United States. Villages have been turned into ghost towns. The young men are gone, and often so are their families, leaving only the elderly to run things. There are a lot of new houses, replacing mud huts, but many stand empty. They were built with money sent from the U.S., but their owners never returned to live there.

Guanajuato is a major "sender" of migrants. It also is a major receiver of remittances. It's had that dubious distinction for decades.

At least 1.5 million people from Guanajuato currently live in the U.S., which ranks the state fourth behind Michoacán, Jalisco and Zacatecas.

In 2005, immigrants sent $1.2 billion in remittances to relatives in Guanajuato, the third highest amount behind Jalisco ($1.3 billion) and Michoacán ($1.7 billion), according to the Bank of Mexico.

While natives are leaving for the U.S., North American tourists are pouring into Guanajuato, at least into the colonial towns. They love the place. They're fascinated with the scenic beauty, the Spanish architecture, the culture and history, as well as agreeable climate.

They flock to the capital Guanajuato, one of Mexico's most beautifully preserved colonial cities, designated a World Heritage Site by UNESCO back in 1988. There they enjoy the cultural offerings of a major university, including the famed annual International Cervantes Festival that draws thousands from all over.

Diego Rivera, Mexico's most renowned artist, was born in Guanajuato. However, as a Marxist in a Catholic bastion, he was persona non grata for years. Former President Vincente Fox is a native son.

The man who followed in Fox's footsteps as governor of Guanajuato, Juan Carlos Romero, has strong connections with the U.S. and Appleton, Wisconsin. Romero met and later married Frances Siekman, who as a Lawrence College Spanish major studied at the University of Guanajuato.

Nearby San Miguel de Allende is the epitome of an American enclave in Mexico. The famed artists' colony and "national monument" is home to at least 5,000 well-to-do Americans, about 10% of the population, for much of the year.

The state of Guanajuato, about three hours north of Mexico City, is bordered by the states of Michoacán, Jalisco, San Luis Potosí and Querétaro. Outside of the colonial corridor, it's a densely populated and diverse region. Its population of nearly five million ranks it sixth, even though it's one of the smallest states in size.

The Spanish *Conquistadores* loved the place, too. It wasn't *El Dorado,* but it was the next best place. They found rich silver deposits, the richest in the world. For more than two centuries, nearly 40% of the world's silver came from Guanajuato.

Guanajuato was one of the first areas in Mexico colonized by the Spaniards back in the early 1520s. Nearly 300 years later, the state of Guanajuato was the first to split with Spain, earning it the title of the "Cradle of Independence."

"*El Grito*," the revolutionary cry for freedom, was issued by a parish priest named Padre Miguel Hidalgo in the village of Dolores on Sept. 16, 1810. The rebel priest gave the Catholic hierarchy fits with his unorthodox beliefs, his lifestyle and his political activism. He questioned the virgin birth and the infallibility of the pope, he gambled, danced and had a mistress and fathered two daughters.

Less than a month after "*El Grito*" was shouted from his pulpit, Hidalgo was excommunicated for "heresy, apostasy and sedition." He was captured by the Spanish and died before a firing squad on July 30, 1811. Ignacio Allende, who had taken control of the rag-tag army, also was killed. Their severed heads were hung in a cage on a Guanajuato street corner for 10 years to serve as a message to future revolutionaries.

Another parish priest, Padre Jose Maria Morelos, assumed command of the rebel forces, and after a decade of sporadic fighting, Mexico finally won its independence from Spain in 1821.

Hidalgo's role in the revolution lasted less than one year. But he's widely revered as a national hero and the father of his country. A state and a city are named for him and his balding image is on the Mexican 1000 peso note.

While the state is better known for its colonial towns, its principal cities are León, Irapuato and Salamanca. León, northwest of the capital, is an industrial center of more than one million people. Irapuato, the region's strawberry grower, is a major hub to the southwest. Salamanca has oil refineries.

The fertile plains amid the mountains, which rise anywhere from 3,000 to 15,000 feet, contain vast farmlands and countless villages. The area, just north of Mexico's central volcanic belt, is called the "*Bajio,*" or lowland.

It's from this agricultural area that a disproportionate number of Mexicans have emigrated to the United States.

The first major wave of emigrants to the U.S. occurred during the revolution of 1910, which took the lives of one million Mexicans and sent another million people north.

But one event that set the stage for millions of Mexicans from Guanajuato and surrounding states to eventually settle in the U.S. was the "Cristero Revolt."

The 1917 Constitution, a result of the Mexican Revolution, aggressively corralled the Catholic Church. The hierarchy had long sided with the wealthy landowners, and the government took drastic steps to put the church in its place.

The new constitution declared the separation of church and state. It outlawed monastic orders, forbad public worship outside of churches, restricted religious property rights and banned priests from politics. There was an uneasy truce between the church and the government until the 1924 presidential election of Plutarco Elias Calles, a strident atheist. He banned the wearing of clerical garb in public. But that was just the start. He then seized church property, expelled all foreign priests, and closed monasteries, convents and religious schools.

The new penal code called for five years in prison for any priest who criticized the government, and just wearing clerical garb in public could result in a fine of $250.

In July 1926, the Mexican bishops responded to those draconian measures by suspending all public worship in Mexico and calling for an economic boycott against the government.

The lines were drawn. The peasants, a people intensely devoted to Our Lady of Guadalupe, and distrustful of the government, sided with the church and took up arms to defend it. Their battle cry was ¡*Viva Cristo Rey!* Long live Christ the King.

The federalists drew their support from urban areas. The militia numbered about 80,000 men. The Cristeros were fervent Catholics from the countryside and small towns. At one time they numbered 50,000 men, along with 10,000 women, members of the Saint Joan of Arc brigade.

The Cristero rebellion lasted nearly three years, with several key battles fought in Guanajuato and surrounding states. U.S. ambassador to Mexico Dwight Whitney Morrow helped negotiate the end of the conflict. On June 27, 1929, church bells rang for the first time since the bishops' edict.

The war claimed the lives of more than 100,000 people, 56,000 on the federal side and about 30,000 Cristeros. After the truce, government forces killed another 5,000 Cristeros. The effects of the war on the church were profound. At least 40 priests were slain. Before the rebellion, there were 4,500 priests; in 1934 there were only 334 priests licensed to serve 15 million people. The others had been eliminated by expulsion, assassination and emigration.

The end of the conflict sent a surge of migrants to the U.S. Tens of thousands of Cristeros and sympathizers from Guanajuato and its neighboring states fled north, with many settling in California. By some estimates, as many as 450,000 migrated to America in the wake of the war..

In the 1940s and 1950s, the U.S. *bracero* work permit program sent millions more to the U.S. to work in the fields. Generation after generation sent its sons and daughters to the United States.

By the turn of the century, at one time there were as many as two million Guanajuato natives living and working in the U.S. An estimated 800,000 lived in Texas, hundreds of thousands more in California and about 240,000 had settled in Illinois.

The number of migrants leaving Guanajuato and nine other central states resulted in half of their municipalities reporting declining populations. Whole villages were depleted, led by El Gusano, which had the highest rate of emigration in Mexico.

The exodus has hit three central Mexican states quite hard. Tens of thousands of migrants leave Jalisco, Zacatecas and Michoacán every year. There currently are more Michoacán natives living in California, Illinois and Texas than in their homeland.

More than half of the natives of Quiringuicharo in Michoacán have moved to Rolling Meadows, a suburb of Chicago. The Mexican village had 4,000 residents in 1995. Eight years later, the population had dropped below 2,000.

Of the 2,200 people who lived in the Michoacán village of Huacao a decade ago, only 400 remain. Nearly all of them are women, children too young to trek across the border, or elderly people who feel too weary.

The village of Casa Blanca in Zacatecas lost 3,300 citizens in the 1990s, with most of them moving to Tulsa, Oklahoma. Fewer than 2,500 remain in the Mexican village.

"Chain migration" is a term used to describe migrants from the same town who create gateway communities for friends and relatives in a new country. Most of the Mexican migrants come from small towns, and most gravitate toward U.S. cities settled by their kinfolk.

Many migrants return to their villages each year for special feasts or to spend the holidays with relatives. They keep connected to their hometowns for the rest of the year via "Casa Guanajuato" enclaves.

When he was governor, Fox initiated a policy of *"acercamiento"* (reconciliation). He created a state office of emigrant affairs to keep in touch with his constituents in the U.S. When he ran for president in 2000, he pledged to be president of all Mexicans, the 100 million in Mexico as well as the millions in the U.S.

He wasn't just looking for votes. He was counting on the emigrants sending home money to help pay for needed community projects. Fox established a *"Tres por Uno,"* program which pledged matching local, state and federal money for each dollar from the U.S.

In 2005, the government financed 92 projects totaling $3.7 million in 32 Guanajuato communities. Of that total, U.S. immigrants contributed $1.1 million.

The village of San José de Mendoza has especially benefited from the benevolence of its former residents. It finally got a new ambulance for its clinic, the school was renovated, and the 300-year-old church got a new roof. A major church reconstruction project, estimated to cost $120,000, is underway.

The 410 immigrant families from San José de Mendoza, who have settled in Phoenix, Salt Lake City and California's San Fernando Valley, raised $35,000 as its share of the project.

The "Three for One" program's stated goal is to create better economic conditions in Guanajuato so fewer people would head to the United States.

So far, the program has only produced deceiving mirages in many villages. Adobe hovels have been transformed into two-story brick houses, crumbling churches have been restored, and new benches and brightly painted litter bins have been placed in town squares. But upon closer inspection, one notices that the houses, pews and park benches are empty.

The Guanajuato farmers who have remained in their fields have had to import workers from southern states as the manpower drain continues to the north. Besides, the locals refuse to work for average Mexican wages. Small assembly plants have been forced to close because they could not find workers who would accept $4-a-day wages.

People feel they can get more money, businessmen lament, by just staying home and awaiting a check from their relatives in the U.S.

---

## Chapter Ten: GUANAJUATO to WI: Among the sources cited:

Chris Hawley, USA Today, "World Focus," Oct. 20, 2008.

Ginger Thompson, The New York Times, "Migrant exodus bleeds Mexico's heartland," June 17, 2001.

Daniel Gonzalez, Arizona Republic, "Immigrants in U.S. revitalize hometowns," Sept. 20, 2006.

Natasha Korecki, Daily Herald, Chicago, "A modern-day ghost town," Nov. 17, 2003.

Wikipedia, "The Cristero war," 2008.

Lonely Planet, Mexico, 1992.

Laura González, University of Texas at Dallas, "Guanajuatense in the U.S.," December 1999.

John Rotel, Book of Augustinian Saints, "Blessed Elias of Socorro Nieves," 2000.

Alexandra Fuller, National Geographic, "Mexico's Pilgrim Cowboys," August 2007.

Amanda Lauer, The Compass, Green Bay, WI, "Defender of faith honored," March 16, 2007.

A group of deported migrants, dressed in black to avoid detection for their night journey, rest in the shade of a parked semi in Nogales, Mexico, awaiting a coyote to guide them in a second crossing to the U.S.

# Chapter Eleven

## *The Journey – 1*

✦

### *Sonora crossroads migrant staging area*

José Luis sat slumped over on a concrete bench in the shadow of Nuestra Señora de Guadalupe Catholic Church and stared at his battered shoes.

He had traveled by foot, by freight train and by third class bus all the way from a tiny but historic town called Comalcalco in the state of Tabasco. It wasn't far from La Venta, the famous religious site of the Olmec civilization, dating back to 1,500 B.C., and its massive heads sculpted from basalt. It wasn't far from the Guatemalan border either.

Comalcalco was home for scores of his kinfolk. Generations had settled along the Bahía de Campeche. Few ever strayed away.

But José Luis did. Here he was in Altar, Sonora, more than 2,000 miles up north. It had taken him two weeks to get there. And his journey was far from over.

He was exhausted. Despondent. He was broke. The *coyotes* had taken his last peso. He could go no further.

He had taken apart his cell phone and was dabbing the panels with a tissue. It had slipped out of his hands and fell into the fountain in the city square as he tried to call his family. He was counting on them to send him money. But the phone wouldn't work.

He was alone. Most of the migrants huddled in the sparse shade of the city square were teenage boys. José Luis was 45. He had never before traveled farther than Veracruz, and that was only a couple of times. He knew the jungles, and the rivers and the low-lying coastal areas along the Gulf of Mexico. But he didn't know the deserts.

In Altar, the noonday breeze felt like a blast furnace. The temperature that day hovered around 105 degrees. Often in mid-summer it reaches 130 degrees, and once 150 degrees was recorded, making the Sonora Desert one of the hottest places on earth.

He took a sip from his plastic liter bottle of water and poured some in the palm of his hand that he cupped to his forehead. He had a headache and a fever, and chills ran through his body.

He had reached the staging area for migrants, the place where as many as 3,000 migrants a day used to gather to contract smugglers to direct and guide them through the security gaps on the U.S. border.

Twice before he nearly made it across the frontier before being turned back by the U.S. Border Patrol. The *coyotes* got their money. But he was nowhere closer to fulfilling the promise he made to his wife the night before she died.

María Guadalupe's health had been fragile almost from the day they were married 20 years earlier. She had a variety of ailments and was sickly since she was a teenager. She suffered a heart attack when she was only 30. Her physician said she was a candidate for bypass surgery. But they lived in a small village, and even in the state capital of Villahermosa, medical facilities were suspect. Mexico City was 600 miles away. But, no matter, they had no money. José Luis sometimes worked as a house painter, but his jobs were few and far between.

The couple had two daughters, Cristina, 18, who recently graduated from secondary school and was about to get married, and Lucía, 13, who after suffering migraine headaches for years, was finally diagnosed as having a brain tumor. The doctors said Lucía's chance for survival and a normal life was dependant on successful surgery. The procedure might cost 100,000 pesos, they said.

María Guadalupe insisted that her husband visit his uncle in the United States. He lived in Florida, had a nice car and house, and on frequent visits to their hometown, he often showed photos and bragged about his connections, and how he could put José Luis into a high-paying job.

José Luis wasn't anxious to leave his village. Other than Uncle Carlos, no one in his family had left home. Yet he knew he could never earn enough in Comalcalco to pay the doctor bills.

It was early May of 2009 when María Guadalupe suffered a second heart attack. There were no ambulances or medical facilities in town. José Luis sensed the end was near. He knelt by her bed, held her hand and placed a wet cloth on her forehead. Haltingly she told him she loved him. Then she made him promise he would go to the U.S. and see Uncle Carlos about that job he had offered. Her mother would take care of the girls while he was away.

She realized she was dying, but she so wanted her daughter Lucía to live.

José Luis had tears in his eyes as he mulled his wife's last words. But sitting alone on a bench in Altar with no money and no friends, he had no idea how he was going to fulfill that promise.

Altar is situated at the crossroads in the Sonora Desert of major highways leading to Nogales and Tucson as well as Mexicali and San Diego. Two decades ago, it was a hot, dusty town that trucks rumbled through on the way to someplace else. There were only two hotels, and together they didn't make one star.

That was before fences went up on the U.S. frontier, and before millions of migrants began to surge along the border, searching for a gap in security to cross into the United States.

The migrant trail began to change dramatically in 1994 with the advent of the North American Free Trade Agreement. By the year 2000, Altar was seeing an average of 2,000 migrants a day. By mid-decade, the numbers soared to 3,000. In the summer of 2009, due to a sour economy in the U.S. and intensified border security, migration through Altar dropped to about 300 a day.

Still, Altar was the major staging area for illegal migration into southwestern U.S.

It's also the headquarters for human as well as drug trafficking. Hundreds of *coyotes* or *polleros* make thousands of dollars guiding migrants across the border. So do the drug cartels and dealers who sometimes pack cocaine in the migrants' backpacks to pay the *coyote's* fees.

Altar's population has soared to more than 8,000, triple that of 15 years ago. Almost everyone is involved in the migrant trade. Retail outlets stock dark, unmarked clothing, backpacks, shoes, and even coated water bottles so they don't reflect lights in the desert. Vendors patrol the streets with racks of assorted garb. Taco stands and cheap eateries abound.

The *zócolo* is the hub of the illicit business. It's there that migrants gather and meet their *coyotes* and await instructions for the 50-mile trip over dusty washboard roads to Sásabe on the border. A lineup of windowless, white vans, with their seats removed in order to pack in as many as 30 migrants, frame the city square, awaiting the *coyote's* signal.

There are now 15 hotels and 80 *casas de huespedes,* mostly over-crowded flop houses, to accommodate the migrants. Many of the guest houses pack dozens of men on triple-stacked cubbyholes in a single room, charging each $5 a night.

At least one *casa* doesn't prey on the migrants. The "Casa de Migrante," supported in part by Catholic Relief Services and the Archdiocese of Hermosillo, offers free-of-charge housing, showers, food, clothes and medical services as well as advice to migrants. Since 2000, it has served 20,000 migrants, mostly single, young men from southern Mexico.

José Luis, sobbing out loud with his head in his hands, was startled when the parish priest tapped him on the shoulder. The priest sat down on the bench alongside him and listened to his story. He had heard a lot of migrant stories. His masses were filled with Mexicans and Central Americans who were on their way to the U.S. The migrants prayed especially hard on the day they were going into the desert.

The priest invited José Luis to stay at Casa de Migrante. It was a haven where he could ponder his next move without being threatened by *polleros* and other predators. Besides, there he could pray to Santo Toribio Romo, the patron saint of migrants, whose portrait was prominent at the *Centro Comunitario*.

Father Romo, who was canonized by Pope John Paul II in 2000, was executed by Mexican militia during the Cristero conflict in 1928. Over the years, his legend has become bigger than life as migrants solicit his spiritual aid when they face dangers in the desert. Many have testified that they have been assisted and rescued by a man, who closely resembles that portrait, who then mysteriously disappears.

José Luis said a prayer in front of the framed photo of Father Romo. He didn't know how he'd get to the U.S., or whether he'd land a good job in Florida, or whether his daughter Lucía would hang on until he made enough money to pay for her operation.

Then he heard his cell phone ring, ever so faintly in his pocket. It was his mother-in-law. She was worried. She hadn't heard from him. She said that Lucia was doing fine.

And yes, she'd somehow find a way to send him the money so he could continue his journey.

# Chapter Eleven

## *THE JOURNEY – 2*

✦

### *Desert claims 5,000 lives in past 15 years*

Most of the Mexican migrants passing through Sonora have never walked through a desert. Most know something about sage brush and cactus, scorpions and tarantulas and snakes, but they don't know what it's like to trudge days in the wilderness under a broiling sun with temperatures reaching 130 degrees and without a water hole or a shade tree in sight.

Migrants come to Altar, halfway between Nogales and Mexicali, from all over Mexico, but a disproportionate number are from Oaxaca and Chiapas, mountainous but temperate climes, with rivers and rain, forests and green fields.

They travel the underground railroad, a series of more than 30 safe houses throughout Mexico, operated by humanitarian groups, notably Maryknoll lay missioners. There they receive lodging, food and information of what lies ahead.

There are warnings posted everywhere of the dangers of the desert, and the human perils of the journey, but still they come to the gateway, hoping against hope to make it to the United States.

The Mexican government distributes brochures which shout in red ink that no one is free of the risk of dying in the desert, that several thousand have perished in recent years, that the *coyotes* lie about the conditions and the distance, saying a jug of water ought to last the two-day trek. The "guides" fail to mention the gangs, thugs, thieves and drug dealers who prey on the desperate migrants, or that young women often become rape victims.

There are handouts that urge migrants to anonymously report the location of corpses they might discover in the desert so they can be recovered, identified and given a proper burial.

In the past 15 years, more than 5,000 migrants have died of dehydration and other causes in the deserts straddling the U.S. frontier. In but the first few months of 2009, the death toll stood at 79 in Arizona alone. Those are just the bodies they've found.

And still they come.

The walls and virtual fences, the surveillance stations and bolstered Border Patrols, and the increased militarization of the U.S. border have funneled millions of migrants to the most desolate and deadly crossings. Sections are fortified when numbers warrant. But it's U.S. border strategy to force migrants to cross inhospitable mountains and deserts, fully realizing that some might die. They're counting on those deaths to be a deterrent to others.

Sásabe, Sonora, the border town long a major magnet for migrants, now has a formidable barrier halting passage to its twin town of Sásabe, Arizona. However, the fence now just forces migrants to skirt the town onto more perilous terrain.

Sásabe was once just a rest stop on a dusty road on the U.S. border. It's now a haven for people making a living smuggling migrants and drugs into Arizona. Its population doubled in recent years to 4,000, and there are hotels and at least a dozen flophouses and restaurants that cater to the illegal border-crossers. A cell phone tower was recently installed on a nearby hill to bolster communication.

The two Border Patrol stations responsible for the area accounted for more than 160,000 of the Tucson Sector's 426,000 apprehensions back in 2005.

Mexican federal officials occasionally raid the village, arresting drug and migrant smugglers. But recently they have been more interested in recovering trucks stolen in Arizona. Besides, the sandy roads leading to Sásabe are an easy giveaway. Large plumes of dust from the official convoys announce their coming an hour before they arrive.

The smugglers play an unending chess game with the Border Patrol. They stand on a hill with binoculars and radios, monitoring the moves of the agents more than a mile away. One smuggler claims he once successfully moved 14 groups of people into the U.S. in a single day. His cut was $100 a person.

Crossing into the U.S. is nearly impossible without a guide. A good *coyote* knows the location of the border cameras. He knows the schedules of the Border Patrol, the changing locations of the checkpoints, as well as the off road trails, gullies and animal trails to be followed.

*Coyotes* also have contracts for vehicle transport from Altar to Sásabe, east and west from Sásabe, and northward from the southern extensions of Tucson, Arizona.

The fees charged by the coyotes vary with supply and demand, as well as circumstances, ranging from $300 to $2,500. Migrants who don't have the money, or can't raise it from relatives, often resort to selling their lands. Sometimes they are solicited to carry drugs across the border as payment, or are forced into indentured labor in the U.S.

Many *coyotes*, and their support networks that provide transportation and housing, have become quite wealthy. Their ill-gotten riches often link them with violent criminal behavior as well as the corruption of government officials. While some believe they're providing a needed service, others don't deny that they just prey on culpable migrants.

Migrants are expected to make the journey in three days. Few do. It's 75 miles from Sásabe to Tucson, when you follow the established roads. Migrants stick to cactus-filled gullies and travel mostly at night.

The Migrant Trail, a journey of solidarity undertaken annually by scores of humanitarians, takes seven days to hike from Sásabe to Tucson. More than 100 participated in the sixth annual "Walk for Life" in May 2009 "to bear witness to the tragedy of death and of the inhumanity in our midst." The participants were accompanied by support vehicles, unlimited food and water, as well as medical attention. Most walkers consumed several liters of water each day, with the temperatures exceeding 100 degrees.

Of course, the migrants don't have it so easy. They're on their own, traveling desert trails like fugitives, ever wary of the Border Patrol, and with only the food and water they can carry.

Some migrants have long-distance *coyote* network connections but most make their first contacts in Altar's *zócolo*, the village's main square. Once arrangements are made, the migrant may spend several days in the plaza awaiting the *coyote's* signal that the trip is filled and the journey is about to begin.

Then the migrant joins as many as 30 others stuffed in a windowless van for the 50-mile trip over a dusty corduroy road to Sásabe. Temperatures reaching 110 degrees are common in the summer months. Upon arriving in Sásabe, the migrants are transferred to pickup trucks that scatter east and west along the Mexican side of the border to the point where they'll be crossing into the U.S.

If a Border Patrol agent spots and pursues the migrants, the *coyote* often abandons the group, which is then scattered in all directions, leaving the migrants to fend for themselves.

Sometimes, the only option that migrants then have is to try to find a road where they may be picked up by the U.S. Border Patrol and returned to Mexico.

While the Border Patrol's white SUVs are the most prominent vehicle on the gravel and baked earthen roads of Southern Arizona, the odds still favor the migrant reaching Tucson. For every 300 migrants apprehended, 1,000 make it through the desert gauntlet.

Southern Arizona consists of hardscrabble lands that have been corralled by barbed wire into massive cattle ranches. Ranchers lease state and federal property to raise a limited number of beef cattle, determined by what the land can sustain. One typical farm of 64 square miles supports only 300 cows.

It's through these sparse desert ranch lands that the migrants trek. It's where they discard their empty plastic water bottles, their torn backpacks, their heavy clothing. It's where some get disoriented, and die of thirst, or of heat stroke, or of hypothermia from the desert's night chills.

Some get violently ill from drinking the stagnant water from the windmill-driven cattle troughs. A gallon jug of water will provide hydration for a day or so in 110-degree heat. Few migrants can carry enough water for three or more days.

A humanitarian group called "Humane Borders" has established more than 70 emergency water stations on U.S. federal lands near frontier with Mexico. Towering blue flags announce the locations of the blue barrels of fresh water. There are a number of groups, including "No More Deaths" and "Borderlinks," which are dedicated to the welfare of migrants.

There are also anti-immigrant groups, most notably one vigilante unit called Minutemen American Defense, which makes news by occasionally patrolling the desert, harassing and detaining migrants and referring them to the Border Patrol. In June 2009 two of its leaders were charged in the murder of a Mexican and his young daughter in a home invasion near Arivaca, Arizona.

The Tucson Sector of the Border Patrol is the busiest sector on the Southwest Border, covering 262 miles of linear border from the Yuma county line to the Arizona-New Mexico state line. It consists of eight stations, with the Tucson station responsible for patrolling the border east and west of Sásabe, Arizona, from the Pozo Verde Mountains to the California Gulch.

More than 400 Border Patrol agents are assigned to the Tucson station. In the past two years, 6,000 agents have been recruited, meeting the national goal of 18,000. Arizona was assigned 800 new agents, bringing its total to 4,100.

The Border Patrol's presence dominates the gravel roads and baked desert trails that delineate the cattle ranchlands. Their white SUVs are everywhere. Each day they apprehend and detain hundreds of migrants crossing the desert. Many are near victims who have been forced to give up their journey and who see the Border Patrol agents as lifesavers.

The Border Patrol has rescued thousands of migrants who might have otherwise perished. In one six-month period, the Tucson Sector counted more than 200 people who were rescued, including two women and their three young daughters who were stranded on the reservation of the Tohono O'odham Nation.

Another group of 14 migrants from Oaxaca, including women and teenagers, were taken to safety when they activated a Border Patrol Rescue Beacon after their *coyote* abandoned them.

The Border Patrol often calls in helicopters to transport victims to hospitals for emergency treatment.

The week of May 7-13, 2009, was typical for the Tucson sector's Border Patrol agents. They rescued 12 migrants, who were without water or food for three days, after one of them placed a 911 call from Hickiwan, Arizona. One was transported via air ambulance to a hospital and was treated for dehydration. The next day they rescued three migrants who were reported lost in the desert near Gila Bend.

In the same week, agents arrested several criminal aliens, including one convicted of manslaughter, as well as known gang members, and seized 1,912 pounds of marijuana, valued at $1.5 million, along with a Chevolet Suburban found abandoned in a wash. They also arrested nine persons near Tucson who claimed armed bandits had robbed them of 14 bundles of marijuana.

The number of migrants detained in the desert and deported to Mexico each year is staggering. Border apprehensions topped 1.6 million in the year 2000. The number dropped significantly in 2008, due to economic and border enforcement factors, as the Border Patrol caught 705,000 migrants. That's still nearly 2,000 a day across the country.

In April 2008, the Tucson Sector agents apprehended 12,434. The same month a year later, a total of 7,262 migrants were detained and deported through the Mariposa Station in Nogales, Mexico.

The agents apprehend individuals and groups in the desert, and transfer them to a waiting bus off the highway, operated by the private security company Wackenhut, which shuttles the migrants across the border to Nogales. Their documents, passports, identification cards and even address books are taken away by the Border Patrol, and the migrants find themselves in a strange city without friends and without money or IDs.

It's all part of the strategy to discourage migrants from again trying to cross the border.

The Mexican Red Cross mans a first aid station at the Mariposa site and U.S. humanitarian groups like "No More Deaths" monitors the migrants' stories and offers half-price bus tickets so they can return home to their families.

Still, many linger about the Mariposa Station, weighing their chances of getting caught by the Border Patrol a second time. They realize that could mean jail, followed by deportation.

Even first timers could face up to 180 days in jail under the Border Patrol's new "enhanced enforcement." It's called "Operation Streamline" at the Yuma, Del Rio and Laredo sectors where selected illegal border crossers get jail time for their first arrests, something that had been reserved for repeat crossers and those with criminal records.

The Tucson Sector, however, in early 2009, targeted just 40 illegal crossers a day for prosecution. The judicial system couldn't handle any more. There's not enough room in the detention centers, nor enough attorneys to defend and prosecute, judges to sentence and law enforcement officials to supervise and transport the border crossers.

In January 2009, the agency averaged 950 apprehensions a day. But even under the Border Patrol's zero-tolerance initiative, desperate migrants believe the risk is worth it. Besides, while some die and many are arrested, most make it to America.

---

## Chapter Eleven: THE JOURNEY: Among the resources cited:

Charles Bowden, Mother Jones, "Border crossers forge a new America," October, 2006.

Brady McCombs, Arizona Daily Star, "BP targeting 40 illegal crossers a day," Jan. 24, 2008.

Claudine LoMonaco, Tucson Citizen, "Border Patrol rescues migrant from well," June 21, 2007.

Thomas Frank, USA Today, "Border detention the lowest since 1976," Dec. 29, 2008.

Michael Marizco, Arizona Daily Star, "Sásabe has turned into a smugglers' haven," Oct. 2, 2005.

U.S. Border Patrol Weekly Blotter, May 7-13, 2009.

Consulado General de Mexico, SRE, "Cuidado Mexicano," 2009 brochure.

Brochures from Humane Borders, Samaritans, No Más Muertes, and Borderlinks.

Graffitti adorns the stark border wall in downtown Nogales, Mexico, symbolizing the two-sided relationship of the migrant to the coyote, the human smuggler, who often has to be relied upon to successfully cross into the U.S.

# Chapter Twelve

## *The Raids-1*

✦

### *The Raid that put Postville on the map*

Enrique remembers well the time and place when his world collapsed.

It was 10 a.m. on May 12, 2008, in Postville, a rural village of 2,273 people in northwestern Iowa, a short drive from the Mississippi River.

It was the day of The Raid.

It was the day when 389 workers, most of them of Mayan descent from Guatemala, were rounded up, declared criminals, sent off to prison and then deported. At the time it was the largest immigration raid by the U.S. Immigration and Customs Enforcement, commonly known as ICE.

It was a massive, coordinated effort to teach the "illegal aliens" a lesson and to send a message throughout the United States that ICE was serious about disrupting the lives of an estimated 12 million undocumented immigrants.

An army of federal police, local and state authorities, 16 agencies in all numbering more than 900 officers, descended upon a kosher meat-packing plant and arrested nearly half of the workforce. Helicopters hovered over AgriProcessors, Inc., the nation's largest kosher slaughterhouse, and a fleet of buses was standing by to transport the shackled employees to the fairgrounds of the National Cattle Congress in Waterloo, Iowa.

Enrique had no idea what was about to happen when he reported for work that Monday morning. He had noticed the helicopter overhead, and there was an eerie stillness around the plant entrance. But then the assembly line suddenly came to a halt, and the workers started yelling "*migra, migra*" as they dashed through the plant, trying to hide.

There had been rumors through the years that the immigration police might raid the plant. It was a known target. AgriProcessors had a track record of multiple workplace violations, and more than three-quarters of its 900 employees were undocumented.

Enrique noticed the plant entrances were all blocked, so he raced up the stairs to the third floor where he hid behind some boxes. Officers found him, and as they were leading him down the stairs, one told him there was nothing to worry about, that it was just a safety inspection.

But then they lined up the workers single file, took their fingerprints and photos, chained their ankles and wrists and corralled them onto a waiting caravan of white buses. For two hours they sat shackled on buses, without knowing the charge or their fate.

Then they were processed at a place meant for cows in Waterloo. Officials interrogated them, one at a time, trying to determine how they got to Postville and how they got their Social Security cards.

ICE officials weren't so concerned with their responses as they were with prosecuting the illegal aliens. It was the first time undocumented immigrants were to face criminal charges. AgriProcessors wasn't an innocent party in all that, but ICE decided the company could wait for its day in court.

ICE had arranged for interpreters, attorneys and magistrates to be brought to Waterloo to fast track the procedures. The immigrants were to be charged with aggravated identity theft, which carried a two-year prison sentence. Or they could accept a plea bargain of five months behind bars for document fraud. Both counts included deportation once the sentence was served.

Enrique, like most of the immigrants, didn't fully understand the charges. Growing up in an indigenous village, his first language wasn't Spanish. He didn't go to school past third grade, and he could barely read or write. But upon the advice of his assigned attorney, he opted for the shorter term. So did all but five of the workers. Enrique figured he would be deported. He didn't expect to first spend five months in prison.

Life was hard growing up in the Guatemala highlands. When Enrique was a boy, he dreamed of becoming a professional soccer player. But he had to drop out of school to work the fields and tend the herd with his father. But then his father became ill and was forced to sell their land. When he died, his family had no place to live. Enrique remembers never having shoes and the many days when there was not enough to eat.

He was the eldest in the family, and he felt responsible for his five siblings. He wanted a better life for them. He wanted them to stay in school.

He knew several people in the village who had gone to work in the United States. They left poor but they returned prosperous. They had fine clothes and new cars and their money built nice homes for their families. His cousin Pedro was one of them. He told Enrique that a person could make more in an hour in the U.S. than he'd earn in a 12-hour day in the fields of Guatemala.

One day a young Mexican man came to the village. He was recruiting workers for a meat-packing plant in Iowa. Enrique figured Iowa was somewhere near Texas. He said the going wage was $7 to $8 an hour, and there would be plenty of overtime pay. He said the border crossings and travel though Mexico weren't all that difficult. And he said he also could provide Social Security cards and other documents if Enrique signed on.

He talked it over with his long-time friend Oscar, and on the day after Christmas the two, both just 18, set out for the United States to live the American dream. Sometimes they took a third class bus, but mostly they walked and they walked through the mountains, through forests, through deserts. They slept by day and walked by night. It took three weeks to reach the U.S. frontier.

There a *coyote* staged their crossing. Enrique and Oscar and 12 other migrants packed the back of a truck in 100-degree heat and headed to the border. They crossed the Rio Bravo on a raft and climbed a tall fence and entered the U.S. Enrique thought he had reached Iowa. It was El Paso, Texas.

The two finally arrived in Postville on a cold, snowy day in February 2007. Enrique had only a light jacket and he was freezing. He checked in at the AgriProcessors plant. The offices were filled with men with long beards, all dressed in black. He figured they must have been at a funeral.

The men were rabbis and the company they ran was the largest kosher slaughterhouse in the country. Hasidic Jews, a branch of Orthodox Judaism, wear distinct clothing and follow strict dietary laws. Back in 1987 the Rubashkim family, along with 200 Hasidic Jews from Brooklyn, New York, took over a defunct meatpacking plant in Postville and turned it into an industrial scale Glatt Kosher operation.

Their arrival, and that of immigrant workers, changed Postville into one of Iowa's most ethnically diverse communities. In the 1990s, the plant employed 700 workers from 14 countries.

At the beginning, AgriProcessors and its hundreds of jobs were seen as a savior to the economically depressed region. Postville's population soared, and business was good. The plant processed $100 million worth of livestock a year.

But soon cultural tensions arose between the Hasidic newcomers and the villagers. And over the years, there came a steady stream of workplace violations: child labor, unsafe working conditions, cruelty to animals, failure to pay wages, hiring undocumented workers and sexual harassment.

In 2006 the company paid a settlement of $600,000 to the Environmental Protection Agency for wastewater pollution violations, and in March 2008, just two months before the ICE raid, it was fined $182,000 for state health, safety and labor violations.

Enrique soon became disenchanted with both the company's pay and working conditions. He regularly worked 14-hour shifts, sometimes as long as 18 hours, often without getting overtime pay. His supervisor treated him badly, denying him breaks and harassing him to work faster. The workers had a half-hour to eat lunch, but that included time to change out of the bloody uniforms, goggles and masks. It was soon time to restart the line, cutting and deveining, quartering and cleaning. It was a tedious routine that was repeated day after day.

Enrique had been on the job for 14 months on the day of The Raid. He was fed up and ready to quit, but he had no other options. He talked with Oscar about going back to Guatemala, but neither wanted to repeat that arduous journey.

That Monday afternoon they sat trembling with fear and shivering from the cold on a bench at the fairgrounds in Waterloo. There were a total of 389 immigrants, mostly Guatemalans but also at least 60 Mexicans, awaiting processing and interrogation. Most assumed they would soon be deported.

Enrique and Oscar agreed that it wouldn't be such a bad ending to their American dream. They'd likely get a free flight back to Guatemala. Besides, they missed their families and friends. They didn't count on lengthy prison sentences before they'd ever get home.

It took just three days to process, interrogate and sentence 297 AgriProcessors' employees. By May 15, most were behind bars in wide range of jails and prisons. Enrique and Oscar were split up. Enrique was sent to a prison in Kansas. He never knew where Oscar ended up.

The now convicted felons were scattered about the country, and some were being transferred to other facilities almost on a monthly basis. When Enrique was told he was going to board a plane in Kansas, he assumed he was being returned to Guatemala. Instead, he ended up in a prison in Miami. Then it was immigration centers and prisons in Virginia, and Oklahoma and Kentucky, before finally being returned to several county jails in Iowa.

After five months behind bars, Enrique was more than ready to go home. But ICE officials had other ideas. Suddenly, their tone and treatment drastically changed. Enrique was free, sort of, with his handcuffs traded for a GPS ankle bracelet. He was given a phone card to call his family. They even bought Enrique a couple of hamburgers at McDonald's in Decorah.

Enrique was ordered to stick around the area. He was to be a key material witness in the criminal prosecution of AgriProcessors' officials. He was given a Green Card so he could work at Luther College in Decorah in the meantime.

Some 235 immigrants --202 Guatemalans and 33 Mexicans -- were deported soon after they completed their prison sentences in the fall of 2008. However, 35 remained in Iowa under GPS constraints, waiting to testify against their employers.

The owner, Sholom Rubashkin, was facing nearly 80 counts of criminal activity. The human resources manager was charged with harboring undocumented aliens for profit and for knowingly accepting fraudulent identification cards. Two Latinos on the company payroll were charged with recruiting "illegal aliens" and for providing them with false documents.

They could get five years in prison and then be deported.

# Chapter Twelve

## *THE RAIDS –2*

✦

### *ICE spends millions to arrest hundreds*

Postville was to be the prototype for future immigration raids conducted by ICE, the U.S. Immigration and Customs Enforcement agency.

It was meticulously planned and orchestrated. ICE officials admitted the coordination and logistical planning efforts had been going on for months before the actual May 12, 2008, raid at AgriProcessors, Inc., the largest kosher meat packing plant in the nation. The Raid also was the largest operation of its type in Iowa.

Sixteen local, state and federal agencies, even including the U.S. Postal Service, totaling more than 900 agents and officers, descended upon a slaughterhouse to capture  suspected undocumented workers. Helicopters hovered in the air and a caravan of white buses lined up nearby. ICE had reserved the National Cattle Congress in Waterloo to process and house the workers. It had called in scores of interpreters, attorneys and magistrates to fast track the prosecution.

In just three days, most of the "illegal aliens" were sentenced and put behind bars.

The cost of the operation?  Officially, more than $5.2 million, not counting transportation and imprisonment fees. However, the total bill to rid Postville of its 389 undocumented workers easily exceeds $10 million, or more than $25,000 per "alien."

ICE put out press releases describing the efficiency of the operation, and lauding its humanitarian efforts. Public Health Service Officers interviewed all those in custody to determine if they had health, caregiver or other concerns. Some 40 workers were thus released -- under supervision -- on humanitarian grounds.

ICE set up a toll-free number that family members could call to obtain information about the custody status and location of those detained. The agency also alerted schools, governmental officials and the Iowa Department of Human Services about the operation the same day.

The announced purpose of The Raid was "to execute a criminal search warrant for evidence relating to aggravated identity theft, fraudulent use of Social Security numbers and other crimes, as well as a civil search warrant for people illegally in the U.S."

The agency leaders thoroughly and competently covered all the bases in a fair and forthright manner. Or so they believed.

"Anyone encountered during this operation who is discovered to be in the U.S. illegally, eventually will be placed into administrative removal (deportation) proceedings," the announcement said, adding that ICE agents already had arrested more than 300 for "administrative immigration violations."

But that's not the charge that faced the immigrants. It wasn't merely a status offense, subject to deportation, but rather a felony, a criminal offense that called for prison time.

The immigrants were charged with "aggravated identity theft," which meant they stole somebody's Social Security card. It carried a two-year prison sentence. But they were offered a plea bargain to speed up the process. If they pleaded guilty to document fraud charges, they'd get five months in prison. All but five agreed to the lesser charge upon the advice of their attorneys.

It was a bogus choice, as the U.S. Supreme Court ruled in May 2009 in an unrelated case. The ruling was issued after the migrants had completed their prison terms and were back in their native countries. In order for "aggravated identity theft" to occur, the court said, the subject must know that the ID belonged to a real person. The workers had no idea who owned the numbers.

The Postville case raised an outcry among immigrant advocates everywhere. A common practice by undocumented immigrants of presenting fake Social Security numbers and other documents to employers had been transformed into federal felonies.

And it was the first time such workers, with no other offenses, received prison sentences.

"ICE is committed to enforcing the nation's immigration laws in the workplace to maintain the integrity of the immigration system," the press release of May 12, 2008 stated. "We carry out that obligation in a fair and responsible manner, ensuring humanitarian needs are taken into consideration."

ICE took pains not to repeat the widely criticized procedures of previous workplace raids, notably those in December 2006 when six meatpacking plants owned by Swift & Co. were targeted. Those raids resulted in 1,297 arrests, including about 100 at the Marshalltown, Iowa, plant.

The agency had thought it had corrected those flaws and had perfected the system. It wasn't prepared for the outrage that erupted throughout the country in the wake of the Postville raid.

Then Iowa Gov. Tom Vilsack blasted the Marshalltown and Postville raids. More than a year later, serving as U.S. Agriculture Secretary, he added his voice to a special commission report that condemned the tactics used by ICE agents.

One of the key certified interpreters brought in from Florida went public with a 14-page report and extensive coverage in the New York Times. He called the Postville judicial proceedings a travesty of justice. Erik Camayd-Freixas said the immigrants were denied due process. Most of the Guatemalans could neither read nor write, and they didn't understand they were facing federal criminal charges, he said. They thought they were in court because they were in the country illegally, not because of Social Security fraud.

Postville was devastated by The Raid. Families were torn apart, and the community, once labeled the "Hometown to the World," was left in ruins.

By the morning of May 13, 2008, one-third of Postville's population had fled, and 120 of the 363 students were absent from school. Some of the students were born in America and thus were U.S. citizens.

Restaurants and businesses were soon forced to close, and there was suddenly a glut of housing. Nearly 40% of the village's workforce was gone. AgriProcessors cut back its production, but by November, the company had filed for bankruptcy.

The community and its churches, notably St. Bridget's Catholic Parish, rallied to the aid and defense of the immigrants. They provided food and clothing and moral support for those left behind who no longer could count on a regular paycheck.

Luther College in nearby Decorah also played a leading role in seeing that Postville and The Raid would not be soon forgotten. Several immigrants who remained in the region to testify in court against AgriProcessors officials produced a play entitled *"La Historia de Nuestras Vidas,"* and noted filmmaker Luis Argueta had a full-length documentary in production about The Raid and its aftermath.

Noble Peace Prize winner Rigoberta Menchu also put the village's plight into national focus through solidarity presentations in Postville.

On the one-year anniversary that put a once, idyllic Iowa town on the map, thousands of people from throughout the U.S. took part in services that both honored the immigrants and decried the U.S. immigration system that fostered The Raid.

But Postville, the classic story of small-town America that was transformed by newcomers and became a media darling for National Geographic Magazine as well as PBS and CNN television series, now is but a melancholic memory.

ICE was created in March 2003 in the wake of 9/11 as an investigative branch of the Department of Homeland Security. It combined the enforcement arms of the former Immigration and Naturalization Service (INS) and the former U.S. Customs Service. Its aim was to more effectively enforce immigration and customs laws and to protect the Untied States against terrorist attacks.

Thousands of illegal aliens have been arrested, jailed and deported over the past five years. Few have had any previous criminal records, and none, to date, have been labeled terrorists.

Workplace arrests by ICE in 2007 were 10 times of what they were in 2002. The total of those arrested for being in the country illegally in 2007 was 4,077, with 863 others charged with criminal violations, such as identity theft. The following year, the number increased 27%, and included 1,103 criminal arrests along with 5,184 administrative arrests.

In August 2008, more than 600 suspected illegal immigrants were detained at a Mississippi transformer plant. It was the largest single-workplace raid in U.S. history. Another 300 workers were rounded up at a chicken processing plant in Greenville, N.C.

The raids have been scattered about the United States, and while the larger operations have received most of the media attention, a number have focused on smaller plants, and on illegal immigrants from countries other than Mexico and Latin America.

Some 28 workers were arrested at an engine manufacturing plant for Japanese cars in Bellingham, Washington in February of 2009. The same month, 138 were arrested, including some from India, at a Van Nuys, California, plant that recycles ink cartridges.

Even the Postville raid, which resulted in the arrests of 290 Guatemalans and 93 Mexicans, included two Israelis and four undocumented immigrants from the Ukraine.

The raids took a huge toll on the companies and communities involved, and, of course, the immigrants themselves, who came to the U.S. desperate to find any kind of work to support their families.

They also carried a huge price tag. Detention costs alone in 2008 were $1.6 billion. ICE's unprecedented decision to prosecute the immigrants criminally rather than in immigration court meant millions of extra dollars to keep the defendants in jail.

To stage a raid, hundreds of agents as well as judges, lawyers and prison officials had to descend often on remote locations. After a raid, ICE herded hundreds of immigrants to distant prisons. In a factory raid in New Bedford, Massachusetts, ICE put 200 workers, shackled head to toe, on chartered airliners and flew them to Texas prisons at a cost of $200,000. Then they had to fly 40 back at additional cost when they were granted release on bail.

ICE became more efficient at deporting workers. It perfected a kind of conveyor-belt justice where immigrants are first charged criminally, then assigned defense attorneys who convinced them to give up their rights for a lesser punishment, after which they are shipped to prisons far from their communities. ICE could carry out the whole process in just 48 hours.

ICE's stated mission is to "protect America and uphold public safety . . . to eliminate the potential threat of terrorist acts against the United States."

However, for the thousands of immigrants arrested and the billions of dollars spent, there have been no reported apprehensions of terrorists or criminals who pose a real threat to the United States. ICE found workers, many of them undocumented but otherwise harmless.

The Bellingham, Washington, raid, may have signaled a new approach to workplace raids. It occurred in February 2009, just a month after Janet Napolitano had taken over as secretary of the Department of Homeland Security. She apparently was caught off guard by the raid, and ordered a review of the procedures.

Meanwhile, the 28 immigrants who had been arrested and taken to immigration detention facilities, were brought back to Bellingham and were given temporary permission to work, pending the outcome of their cases.

There were no more major ICE workplace raids that year.

The DHS in May 2009 announced new guidelines for immigration enforcement. It was to focus on the criminal prosecution of employers who knowingly hire people who lack permission to work in the United States "in order to target the root cause of immigration."

"ICE will continue to arrest and process for removal any illegal workers who are found in the course of these worksite enforcement actions," the DHS statement said. However, the target had shifted from workers to employers. And in addition, ICE headquarters had to be in the know before any workplace raid could take place.

---

**Chapter Twelve: THE RAIDS: Among the resources cited:**

Tony Leys,  Des Moines Register, "ICE raid tactics blasted by panel," June 18, 2009

Patricia Zapor, National Catholic Reporter, "Court rulings signal changes for immigrants," May 15, 2009.

Adam Liptak, The New York Times, "Justices limit use of identity theft law," May 5, 2009.

Luis Argueta, documentary, "AbUSed – The Postville Raid," April 2009.

Postville workers, presentation of "La Historia de Nuestras Vidas," Decorah, Iowa, March 15, 2009.

Loret Turnbull, The Seattle Times, "Immigration Officials raid Bellingham plant," Feb. 24, 2009.

Robert Hildreth, New America Media, "Ice immigration raids waste time and money," Dec. 26, 2008.

Mitch Weiss, Associated Press, Greenville, S.C., "300 suspected illegal immigrants caught in raid," Oct. 6, 2008.

Emily Bazar, USA TODAY,  "Citizens sue after immigration raids," June 24, 2008.

U.S. Immigration and Customs Enforcement, news release, May 12, 2008.

The Economist of London, England,  Austin, Texas, "Immigration: Not very nICE," May 2, 2008.

National Geographic, "In Postville, Iowa, kosher is kosher," June 2005.

# *Plane wreck at Los Gatos*

Folk song lyrics, written by Woody Guthrie in 1948 and performed by Pete Seeger, commemorating those migrants who died in a plane crash while being deported to Mexico.

*"The crops are all in and the peaches are rott'ning,*
*The oranges piled in their creosote dumps,*
*They're flying 'em back to the Mexican border*
*To pay all their money to wade back again."*

*CHORUS*
***"Goodbye to my Juan, goodbye, Rosalita***
***Adios mis amigos, Jesús y María***
***You won't have your names when you ride the big***
***airplane,***
***All they will call you will be "deportees."***

*"My father's own father, he waded that river,*
*They took all the money he made in his life;*
*My brothers and sisters come working the fruit trees,*
*And they rode the truck till they took down and died.*

*"Some of us are illegal, and some are not wanted,*
*Our work contract's out and we have to move on;*
*Six hundred miles to that Mexican border,*
*They chase us like outlaws, like rustlers, like thieves.*

*"We died in your hills, we died in your deserts,*
*We died in your valleys and died on your plains.*
*We died 'neath your trees and we died in your bushes,*
*Both sides of the river, we died just the same.*

*"The sky plane caught fire over Los Gatos Canyon,*
*A fireball of lightning, and shook all our hills,*
*Who are all these friends, all scattered like dry leaves?*
*The radio says, "They are just deportees."*

*Is this the best way we can grow our big orchards?*
*Is this the best way we can grow our good fruit?*
*To fall like dry leaves to rot on my topsoil*
*And be called by no name except "deportees?"*

# Chapter Thirteen

## *The Deported*

✦

### *After 12 years in U.S., he's sent packing*

○ ○ ○ ○ ○ ○ ○ ○ ○ ○ ○ ○ ○ ○ ○ ○ ○ ○ ○ ○ ○ ○ ○ ○ ○ ○ ○ ○ ○ ○ ○ ○ ○ ○

Rogelio worked the orange groves of California. He also tended the fields of Oregon. And he groomed the flower gardens of the rich in Seattle.

For the past 12 years, by the sweat of his brow and the ache of his back, he labored to live the American dream. At last, he was about to start up his own landscaping company.

And then he was deported.

In the morning, he was the boss. By noon, he was an "illegal alien." The next day, he was behind bars in Eloy, Arizona, a giant detention facility, awaiting an U.S. Immigration and Customs Enforcement (ICE) shuttle across the border to Nogales, Mexico.

He was just 16 when he first crossed the border and the desert on his way to L.A. He had finished *secundaria* school the week before, and he and his best buddy, Tomás, decided that they weren't going to spend the rest of their lives in San Blas, Nayarit.

San Blas was an historic town, a key Spanish port on the Pacific that dates back to the late 16th century. Rogelio was a good student. He even could recite by heart Longfellow's "Bells of San Blas," a poem that was etched on a brass plaque in front of the centuries-old church that commands the village square.

He knew all about Father Junípero Serra, the Spanish Franciscan friar, who in 1768 set out from San Blas to establish the 21 missions that stretch throughout California.

Rogelio liked history, especially the past that connected his hometown to the United States. He dreamed of going to California someday to visit San Juan Capistrano -- on his way to Hollywood. Someday he'd stop at the mission in Monterey where Father Serra was buried – on his way to San Francisco.

It was early June of 1997 when Rogelio and Tomás boarded a bus for Tijuana. They figured they would get a job doing something, somewhere, preferably in Los Angeles. They didn't give much thought of how they were going to cross the border, either. Thousands and thousands of Mexicans had done it before, Rogelio said. It couldn't be that hard.

They didn't take into account "The Tortilla Wall," a 10-foot fence of welded steel that started in the Pacific Ocean and ran 14 miles to the Otay Mesa Border Crossing. It was among the first border barriers in 1993, and it effectively altered the entry point of undocumented immigrants into the U.S. The year before, more than 200,000 were apprehended at the border. The year after, the numbers dropped to just 9,000.

The Wall didn't stop the immigrants, of course. It just moved them farther east along the frontier into the Imperial Valley. The two teens were told to make their way to Mexicali, where they'd contact a *coyote* who would help them cross over to Calexico, California, and then onto El Centro.

The temperatures hovered above 100 degrees in the desert as they approached an irrigation canal, part of the All-American Canal network which, with the help of the Colorado River, waters 500,000 acres of Imperial Valley cropland.

The water seemed a mirage, but it was refreshingly real as Rogelio dove in. Tomás hesitated. He wasn't a good swimmer. Rogelio insisted. They had to cross the canal anyway. Tomás stepped off the concrete ledge, and the current immediately carried him downstream.

Rogelio got out of the water and ran franticly alongside the canal wall, but he couldn't see his friend in the murky flow. Finally, as the current ebbed, Tomás' lifeless body floated to the surface.

Rogelio didn't know what to do. He hollered for help but there was no one around for miles. Earlier he had seen a U.S. Border Patrol car near a branch of the Westside Main Canal. He didn't want to leave his best friend in the desert, but he didn't want to get caught by the *migras*, either.

He took out a pencil and a piece of paper from his backpack and wrote Tomás' name, hometown and his parents' telephone number. He said a prayer, put his Our Lady of Guadalupe medal and the note in Tomás' pocket, and with tears in his eyes, whispered *adiós*.

Rogelio made it to Brawley before sundown, hitchhiked a ride with a truck driver early the next morning and arrived in Escondido. There he found a telephone, and he called Tomás' mother.

Once again, he didn't know what to do. Should he scrap his dream and go back to San Blas? Or should he go it alone?

He was troubled, even after he made his decision to at least make it to Los Angeles. There he got a job as a gardener for a wealthy family. After six months, he became restless and headed north. He had been told that his mother had died, and that his older sister had gotten married and had moved to Mexico City.

There was no one back in San Blas that he wanted to see.

From Bakersfield, he moved to Monterey, and then to San Francisco, picking up odd jobs along the way. He continued north to Portland, Oregon, and then to Seattle, Washington.

There he decided to settle down. He found a girlfriend. A blonde, blue-eyed beauty. After six months of dating, they moved in together. Her parents strongly objected to their daughter taking up with a Mexican immigrant. They figured the affair would soon end and their daughter Jill would realize she had made a big mistake.

Jill was more stubborn than her folks. She wasn't about to give in, even though she had early misgivings about Rogelio. Besides, he was quite handsome, and her girlfriends were jealous.

Their first child was a brown-eyed boy; they named him Tommy. Their second, two years later, was another brown-eyed boy who they named Roger. Rogelio was ecstatic. Jill wasn't. She wanted a daughter, a mirror image. But she didn't want to go through childbirth again, and she wasn't about to adopt.

Rogelio was a hard worker. He was the gardener for a large estate, but he also moonlighted for a landscaping firm. He took a couple of classes in horticulture at a technical school. He was getting ready to be his own boss someday.

The boys adored their father, and he was doting dad. Rogelio, whose English was quite good by that time, taught his sons to speak Spanish. He played baseball with them and when the boys reached ages five and seven, he volunteered to be their soccer coach.

While the boys grew closer to their dad, Jill and Rogelio grew farther apart. Her parents wanted her to dump him. Some days she thought it a good idea. Following a spat one evening, she called the police and claimed that he had threatened her. Rogelio denied the charge, but he didn't challenge it for fear that his immigration status would be revealed. Jill went ahead and got a restraining order.

Rogelio felt his girlfriend – they didn't talk about marriage – would relent and they'd soon be reconciled. He spent the next two nights in a cheap motel. But there was a soccer game that Saturday, and the coach's son Tommy was the team leader. Rogelio stopped by to pick him up, and as he entered the door, Jill was on the phone.

She didn't call the police. She called immigration. She said her former boyfriend was an illegal alien and he had violated a restraining order. Within minutes, he was in custody. ICE agents weren't interested in the violation. They just pushed through the process of deportation.

The following day, Rogelio, in handcuffs, was on a plane bound for Tucson. By nightfall, he was in Eloy, Arizona, in the massive, 1,500-bed detention facility operated by Corrections Corporation of America. By the end of the week, he had been shuttled across the border to the Mariposa station in Nogales, Mexico.

He had no papers, no identification. They had even taken his address book with the phone numbers of friends and family. He hadn't been to Nogales before. He walked the streets and along the towering, steel grid wall that divided the downtown from the U.S. The rusty panels, standing on end, were used during the first Gulf War to create landing strips in the Iraq deserts.

Rogelio stood on the curb of the busy street and looked up at the 16-foot wall, topped with barbed wire, and laden with graffiti, including creative sculptures of coyotes. As he walked along the wall, he could catch glimpses of buildings on the other side.

He didn't know what to do. He missed the boys. Yet he knew if he was caught crossing to the other side, he wouldn't just be deported. He'd do time in prison. He might never see his sons again.

He got on a bus heading to Altar, a Sonora desert crossroads town. He knew it was a staging outpost for Mexicans heading to the U.S. Some days as many as 3,000 migrants would pass through the town to be guided by *coyotes* through the Sásabe border crossing.

Rogelio wasn't anxious to return to his hometown of San Blas. He had no family there, and after a dozen years in the U.S. without contact, his friends were few.

He sat on a stone bench in the town zócolo, a shady oasis in the blistering heat, and tried to weigh his options. He thought of his best buddy, Tomás, and how he longed to see Los Angeles. He wondered if his body had ever been recovered.

He thought of his son Tommy and how the nine-year-old loved to play soccer, and how they'd hug when he scored a goal. Maybe Jill would have a change of heart, and take him back. Then again, maybe she would call immigration.

Rogelio watched as a white van across the plaza was being packed with migrants. He knew that most of them would make it across the border that day. Most of them would make it through the desert. Most of them would find jobs and a better life in the U.S.

The *coyote* paused before closing the back doors on the van. He saw Rogelio staring in the distance. There was room for one more, he said.

Tomorrow, Rogelio said. Maybe tomorrow.

# Chapter Thirteen

## *The Deported – 2*

✦

## *It cost $2.4 billion to detain, deport 'aliens'*

It's big business, this roundup of "illegal aliens" in order to protect the nation from terrorists. And it's growing by leaps and bounds.

The 2009 fiscal budget for the U.S Immigration and Customs Enforcement agency totals $5.9 billion. That includes $2.4 billion for detention and removal operations.

Four years earlier, the budget totaled $3.5 billion, with $1.2 billion set aside to handle immigrants without papers.

The numbers are stunning, especially for an agency that's just six years old.

ICE has more than 17,000 employees on its payroll. That doesn't count the contracted workers, the private corporations running detention centers or law enforcement officers and county jails that assist apprehending the undocumented across the nation.

There now are 33,400 beds available in more than 300-ICE managed detention and processing centers, compared to 18,500 in 2003. There are 14 major centers, from San Diego to New York City, and from Tacoma to Puerto Rico.

One of the largest detention facilities is in Eloy, Arizona, where Corrections Corporation of America has room for 1,500 migrants. Eloy is in the desert west of Tucson and its claim to fame, before immigrants came, is that it's the home of the world's largest skydive drop-zone. However, its biggest business by far is Corrections Corporation of America. The town's 2005 census population of 10,855 even includes CCA's prisoners.

ICE's annual report for fiscal 2008 has a long list of accomplishments that include:

--356,739 illegal aliens removed from the U.S., up 23%.

--221,085 criminal aliens in federal prisons on the way, up 46%.

--34,155 fugitive aliens rounded up for deportation, up 6%.

--200,000 removed by ICE's flight operations unit, up 20%.

ICE was created in March 2003 as the largest investigative branch of the Department of Homeland Security. It combined the law enforcement arms of the former Immigration and Naturalization Service and the former U.S. Customs Service.

Its annual report covers prosecution of a vast variety of criminal activities ranging from human smuggling (2,138 arrests) to child sexual predators (1,140 arrests); and from narcotics trafficking (8,396 arrests) to transnational gangs (3,865 arrests).

But while the stated goal of ICE's mission is to "protect America and uphold public safety," its most singular task has been focused on ferreting out "illegal aliens."

ICE made 6,287 arrests of undocumented workers in a series of worksite raids in 2008. The number was 27% greater than the previous year.

ICE also energized a program to involve local law enforcement in outing undocumented migrants. In 2008, ICE received 807,000 queries from officers in the field as to the immigration status of aliens held in police custody. It was an increase of nearly 11% from the previous year.

Its 287(g) program gives limited immigration enforcement authority to participating state and local law enforcement agencies. Some 67 agencies signed up and those agreements have resulted in nearly 74,000 aliens being identified for deportation from the U.S. since 2006.

ICE also provided training in 2008 to more than 12,000 federal, state and local law enforcement officers in investigative techniques that help identify potential cases.

ICE sees that "force-multiplier" approach as the way of the future. It aims to develop and enhance such partnerships and reduce the boundaries that have traditionally separated law enforcement agencies.

While the involvement of local police in immigration issues is considered an efficient and cost-effective way to round up undocumented immigrants, it does come at a cost. Trust is compromised. Immigrants are less likely to cooperate with local police if they're also working for the *migras*. There's also a greater fear of racial profiling, and of detaining suspects without cause.

Some sheriff departments have enthusiastically signed up for training in the 287(g) program and have referred thousands of illegal aliens to ICE for deportation, once they have completed jail sentences for minor offenses.

Other local police agencies have refused to take part in the roundup operation, fearing it would jeopardize their relationship with the immigrant community, and preferring to leave all immigration issues to the feds.

They see immigration violations as civil, not criminal. Immigrants detained during this process are in non-criminal custody of the Department of Homeland Security (DHS).

About half of all immigrants held in detention have no criminal record. Others may have committed some crime in their past, but they have already paid their debt to society. They're detained for immigration purposes only.

It's estimated that by the end of 2009, the U.S. government will have held 440,000 people in immigration custody, nearly three times the number a decade ago, at a cost of $1.7 billion. In 2001, fewer than 95,000 were detained but by 2007, the number had risen to 300,000.

The average daily population of detained immigrants has grown from 5,000 in 1994 to 32,000 at the end of 2008. The U.S. Congress has already authorized the creation of more detention beds, which will bring the capacity to nearly 62,000.

ICE's stated goal is to deport all removable aliens by 2012.

Today's detention system originated in the United States' response to mass migrations, particularly that of Cubans, Haitians and politically displaced Central Americans, in the early 1980s.

In the 1990s, the U.S. made a major shift in immigration policy, using detention as a primary means of enforcement, regardless of whether the individual was a flight risk or serious risk to society. In 1996, the Congress passed legislation that dramatically expanded the use of mandatory detention without bond.

The 1996 laws also established a new procedure called "Expedited Removal," that allows immigration inspectors to summarily remove immigrants arriving without proper documentation. This is done without a hearing, and detention is mandated for the time it takes to remove that person from the U.S. Originally, Expedited Removal was required only at the border, but in 2006, it was expanded to include all areas within 100 miles of U.S. borders.

The time behind bars in detention facilities varies case by case, but the average stay is now about 30 days, down from 89 days when ICE first came on the scene in 2003.

ICE's detention system is a multi-billion-dollar industry, driven in large part by corporations and even public institutions, like county jails.

Revenues and stock prices are soaring for private prison companies that build immigration prisons, like Corrections Corporation of America (CCA) and the GEO Group, Inc. These companies have an incentive to urge the government to build more jails and they regularly lobby in Washington, D.C., for more detention facilities.

The first private prison in the U.S. was an immigration detention center. In 1983, CCA landed a federal contract to build a facility in Houston, Texas. Before it was even finished, CCA began detaining immigrants in rented motel rooms.

The Houston Processing Center and a similar facility in Aurora, Colorado, which was owned by GEO Group and operated by Wackenhut, both opened in 1984.

There are about 400 facilities across the country used by the Department of Homeland Security to detain immigrants. Only eight of those are ICE-owned and operated. In addition, ICE contracts with more than 300 local or county facilities through intergovernmental agreements, private prison corporations and the federal Bureau of Prisons.

Private companies and local governments vie for contracts to expand ICE detention bed space. They are paid an average of $95 a day per bed. DHS also buys bed space from a hodgepodge of 312 county and city jails scattered throughout the country. Two out of every three immigrants spend some time in those institutions.

As detentions have skyrocketed, so have deportations. In 2008, a total of 356,739 people were deported to their native lands. The year before, the number was 288,663 and in 2004 there were only 174,000 deportations.

For fiscal 2009, ICE is projecting 400,000 deportations, and estimates the cost to remove them from the U.S. at up to $3 billion.

ICE partnered with local police in 2008 to find and remove 114,000 "criminal aliens," illegal immigrants who have committed any kind of offense, including misdemeanors. Some 85,000 of those were Mexican nationals.

While many Americans believe that immigration offenses are often linked to criminal behavior, less than one per cent of all foreign-born people in the U.S. have ever been incarcerated.

Still, the Department of Homeland Security sees the need to check out all those foreigners in county jails throughout the nation. The "Secure Communities" program, which began in 2008 as a pilot study, will expand to all the country's jails by 2013.

It will allow law enforcement officials to automatically match fingerprints against federal immigration databases. Those in the U.S. without authorization will face deportation when they have completed their jail terms.

ICE estimates the number of incarcerated criminal aliens in the U.S. at between 300,000 and 450,000 people.

Currently, everyone arrested and booked into a local jail is fingerprinted, and the prints are run through the FBI's criminal history database. If local police want an immigration check, DHS personnel have to search their records manually. In 2008, only 10% of the inmates in the country's 3,000 local jails had their immigration status checked.

Since October 2008, the program has operated on a trial basis in dozens of counties around the U.S. and in such cities as Dallas, Boston, Houston, Miami and Phoenix. Police officers fingerprint inmates and automatically query the prints through both DHS and FBI databases.

The system, however, does not identify those who have never been fingerprinted by government authorities.

---

## Chapter Thirteen: THE DEPORTED: Among the sources cited:

U.S. Immigration and Customs Enforcement, "Detention Management," annual report FY-2008.

Independent Media Center, "List of U.S. Immigration Detention Facilities," April 26, 2006.

Mark Dow, "American Gulag," University of California Press, Berkeley, 2004.

Detention Watch Network, "About the U.S. Detention and Deportation System," 2009.

Jennifer Ludden, National Public Radio, "ICE eyes 400,000 deportations," July 15, 2009.

Alex Kingsbury, US News, "Immigration checks on criminals could increase deportations," May 27, 2009.

John Schwartz, The New York Times, "Bush rule bolstering deportations is withdrawn," June 3, 2009.

The Sirens Chronicle, "ICE deported 349,041 immigrants during the 2008 fiscal year," Nov. 9, 2008.

A cowboy on horseback delivers milk throughout Citlaltépec, Veracruz, a small, remote village that once was the center of a large cattle ranch about 100 miles south of Tampico on the Gulf coast.

# Chapter Fourteen

## *In The U.S. Of A. -1*

✦

### *The poor can't get a visa to visit the U.S.*

○ ○ ○ ○ ○ ○ ○ ○ ○ ○ ○ ○ ○ ○ ○ ○ ○ ○ ○ ○ ○ ○ ○ ○ ○ ○ ○ ○ ○ ○ ○ ○ ○ ○ ○ ○ ○

**The New Colossus**

*Not like the brazen giant of Greek fame,*
*With conquering limbs astride from land to land;*
*Here at our sea-washed, sunset gates shall stand*
*A mighty woman with a torch, whose flame*
*Is the imprisoned lightning, and her name*
*Mother of Exiles. From her beacon-hand*
*Glows world-wide welcome; her mild eyes command*
*The air-bridged harbor that twin cities frame.*
*"Keep ancient lands, your storied pomp!" cries she with silent*
*lips.*

*"Give me your tired, your poor,*
*Your huddled masses yearning to breathe free,*
*The wretched refuse of your teeming shore.*
*Send these, the homeless, tempest-tost to me,*
*I lift my lamp beside the golden door."*

**Emma Lazarus 1883**
**Statue of Liberty plaque has greeted**
**millions of immigrants to the U.S.**

Leticia is a U.S. citizen now. But she hasn't forgotten her country. She'll always be a Mexican.

It was hard for her to stand up in the federal courtroom in Milwaukee, Wisconsin, and raise her right hand and denounce her allegiance to the land of her fathers.

She thought of her grandfather, Alejandro, who had recently died. She couldn't be there for his funeral. He was a peasant, but he was proud to be a Mexican. When Leticia was a young girl, he'd prop her on his knee and tell her all about his father and his grandfather, too, and how the family once ruled a large cattle ranch and lived in a hacienda.

They lived in a different time, but in the same town. Generations of Santiagos have called Citlaltépec home. Few have ever left, for long.

Leticia left, but she keeps coming back. The ranch is gone, and so is the hacienda. But her mother and father, her brothers and sisters, aunts and uncles and cousins by the dozens are still there.

She was the first to go to the U.S.

After finishing middle school, and after celebrating her *quinciñera*, the highlight of all teenage Mexican girls, she followed in the steps of her big sister Mónica. There was nothing to do in Citlaltépec, a remote village in the Sierra Madre Oriental foothills of northern Veracruz, except get married, and Leticia had this distant dream of seeing the world first.

She made it as far as Mexico City and worked as a servant for several wealthy families. One was especially mean to her. At Mónica's urging, she applied for a job in the household of Claudio X. Gonzalez. He was president of Kimberly-Clark of Mexico and he and his wife lived in a mansion in the tony neighborhood of Lomas de Chapultepec, once the summer residence of Aztec nobles.

Leticia had grown up, along with her five siblings, in a three-room shack, with no running water, off and on electricity, and an outside shed with a stick-fed brazier that served as the kitchen stove. Their diet consisted of beans and tortillas, and on very special occasions, chicken tacos or enchiladas.

She knew nothing of wealth. There were no rich people in Citlaltépec. There used to be a few when the town was the heart of a huge ranch. But that was several generations ago.

Leticia was one of eight household servants. There were chauffeurs and security guards, butlers, cooks and maids and cleaning women. Leticia broke in by polishing the silver every day. It was her only job.

Gonzalez had been chief executive of Kimberly-Clark de Mexico ever since 1973 and was largely responsible for the company's success. In the mid-1990s, with sales of over $1 billion, K-C produced more than half of Mexico's paper products. In 1997 he had an estimated net worth of $200 million.

He has been ranked as the sixth most important entrepreneur in Mexico. From 1988 to 2000, he was a chief advisor to two Mexican presidents, Carlos Salinas de Gortari and Ernesto Zedillo.

Gonzalez also supervised all of K-C's Latin American operations and served on the parent company's board of directors, which regularly gathered in Neenah, Wisconsin.

And that became Leticia's link to the United States.

When Gonzalez's son Pablo and his wife Ana were sent to Neenah in 1996 to learn the ropes of K-C's international operations, Leticia was asked to accompany them as the nanny for their two small children. She also was to be their maid and cook.

When they vacationed and traveled by private jet, she went along. She got to see the world, or at least some of it while changing diapers.

After two years in Neenah, Pablo and his family returned to Mexico City. Leticia went with them. Her visa, as a domestic servant, was linked to theirs. She had no life of her own, and that started to grate on her.

She lived well, ate well and traveled well but she was not free. She was at their beck and call, around the clock, with precious little time to herself. She realized it was different for servants in America, but after 10 years of working for Mexican families, she knew it just wasn't the life for her.

If she had to, she'd rather join her mother in sewing children's clothes and travel from market to market in rural Mexico selling the items. But what she really wanted to do was to go back to school. She had only completed ninth grade in Citlaltépec.

The Gonzalezes agreed to pay her tuition, helped her to secure a student visa and in the winter of 1999 she was back in Wisconsin and enrolled at Fox Valley Technical College in Appleton. She joined a group of promising but impoverished students from Central America and the Caribbean in a special two-year business program.

When she started, she knew but a few words of English. But two years later, she was quite fluent and she graduated with high honors and a grade point of 3.85. Her mother and father, and older brother Miguel Angel secured visitor visas and proudly attended the ceremonies. It was the first time anyone in their family had graduated from college. No one had even completed high school.

It was the first and last time anyone in her family was allowed to come to the United States. Three months later, 9-11 also changed their world. The threat of terrorism effectively canceled visas for the poor.

One day Leticia met a young American who liked Mexican food, spoke a few phrases in Spanish, and tried to teach her English. They hit it off from the start. Several years later, they got married, first before a judge in Appleton to ease immigration requirements, and then in Mexico. Leticia insisted she really wouldn't feel married until she walked down the aisle of San Nicolás Church where she and all of her family had been baptized.

The church got a new coat of whitewash and the town was abuzz for the wedding that united two cultures. They killed the fatted calf – actually it was a 800-pound steer – and served *barbacoa* to 1,200 people, most of the village as well as some from surrounding towns.

Leticia was happy to be among her people. If she had her way, she'd stay in Citlaltépec. But her husband had a good job back in Wisconsin. There was no work in her village.

So they went back to the Fox Valley, bought a house and furnished a guest room for when her mother might visit. Leticia and her husband spent their vacations each year in Citlaltépec. But no one from the village was able to visit them in Neenah.

She got a part-time job teaching Spanish at St. John's School in Little Chute. She enjoyed the children and the classes, but most of all, it offered her an opportunity to do something for her village. Every year the students raised money to send to the missions, and the children of Citlaltépec became that mission.

At first a few thousand dollars bought a computer and a television set for Leticia's former middle school. St. John's Parish got involved, and then the entire community of Little Chute joined in the campaign, and over the next seven years the donations soared. Families sponsored scores of poor children who couldn't attend school because they didn't have shoes or uniforms or even pencils and notebooks.

Leticia's family, especially her mother and her sister Mónica, coordinated the program which had grown to nearly $10,000 a year. Leticia's annual home visit was spent purchasing and distributing the gifts to the schools, the church and to nearly 100 needy children.

Her links with Little Chute had made her something of a hero in her hometown.

She was honored by her alma mater, Alfonso Arroyo Flores *Secundaria*, at a special convocation. A plaque in her name, noting that she had gone on from Citlaltépec, but she had never forgotten her village, was installed in the school lobby.

She was pregnant that fall, and more than anything she wanted her mother Lucía to be at her side when she gave birth. Leticia and her husband prepared the packet of documents to be presented with the visitor's visa application. An appointment was made with the U.S. Embassy in Mexico City, three months in advance.

Her mother boarded a bus for the eight-hour trip to Mexico City, stayed overnight on the couch of a friend's house, and arrived early the next day at the American embassy – where she waited six hours to be called by number. The agent had a large envelope containing the documents on his desk, but he didn't bother to sort through them. He looked up at Lucía and simply said, "Application denied."

Lucia was stunned. Leticia was devastated. No explanation was given. There was no way to appeal. An immigration counselor in Wisconsin told Leticia to try again, but next time to change her mother's status. Important people get visas, she said.

St. John's had a "sister school" relationship with the *secundaria* in Citlaltépec, and St. John's Church had a "sister parish" connection with San Nicolás. Since the entire Little Chute community had become involved in supporting Citlaltépec, there was interest in linking the two municipalities under the Sister Cities International program.

Both village boards were enthusiastic about the proposal, voting unanimously to become "sisters." Committees were formed in Little Chute and in Citlaltépec, and both governments were anxious to begin exchange programs.

Leticia was determined to try again to get her mother to visit Wisconsin and to see her grandson. Lucía, who had coordinated St. John's mission project for more than five years, had been named chairman of the Citlaltépec "Sister Cities" committee.

This time, Leticia wasn't going to take any chances. She packed an envelope with endorsements from Sister Cities International, the two U.S. Senators from Wisconsin along with the two Fox Valley representatives, documents of financial support and responsibility and an official invitation for Lucia from the Little Chute Village Board.

Lucia boarded that eight-hour bus ride, found a place to stay in Mexico City, got to the U.S. Embassy early the next day, waited eight hours for her number to be called, and faced the same agent. He looked up at Lucía and simply said, "Application denied."

Lucía was humiliated. She had been turned down two times in one year. She wasn't going to try again. The agent didn't say so, but Leticia later learned her mother's visa application had been denied because poor people are seen at risk to remain in the U.S. She had a husband, five children, six grandchildren, a house and a cottage business in Citlaltépec. But that wasn't deemed enough to guarantee her return. She didn't have a big bank account.

On the same day when thousands of Mexicans would illegally cross into the U.S. without any papers, a middle-aged grandmother who had submitted fingerprints and a packet of supportive documents was denied entrance to the U.S. to visit her daughter and grandson for a two-week period.

Lucía could have entered the U.S. illegally like the rest, hiring a *coyote* to guide her across the border. But Leticia would have none of that. She was sympathetic toward undocumented migrants. She befriended many. She could empathize with their plight.

But she couldn't understand why her mother wasn't allowed to visit her grandson. She had Mexican friends, with legal papers, who regularly had their parents as houseguests. But they were able to secure U.S. visas because they were wealthy. Lucia was poor.

Leticia knew that someday she would become a U.S. citizen. Still, she hesitated. She felt she would be a traitor to her family and her country. But then she was told that once she became a citizen, she could petition for her mother to come to the U.S.

That did it. She requested the application papers, studied the questions, passed the test, and in February 2008 she raised her right hand in the Milwaukee federal courthouse and became a U.S. citizen.

Leticia had another motivation for becoming a citizen. She was upset at the treatment of her people. Migrants were being demonized, and the political campaigns were getting nastier.

She heard the message of a man who promised to change all that. And she wanted to be able to vote for him.

Leticia, like the vast majority of the growing Hispanic community, went to the polls that November and proudly cast her ballot for Barack Obama.

It may take years, but at least there's a good chance that someday her mother may be granted a visitor's visa to hug her now two grandsons in America.

# Chapter Fourteen

## *In The U.S. Of A. – 2*

✦

### *Millions of Mexicans are in the U.S. to stay*

Latinos sent a forceful message to the nation in November 2008 that they had become a major political force to be reckoned with, now and in the future.

Two out of every three Hispanic votes were cast for Barack Obama. And he wasn't even their first choice. Hillary Clinton was their favorite in the primaries. The Democratic Party won, and will likely continue to command the lion's share of the Latino vote -- unless the Republican Party begins to respect the power if not the opinions of the fastest growing minority in America.

President Obama owes his victory to the recognition of the needs and numbers of the immigrant community. The Republicans lost on an ill-conceived move to rally reactionaries against immigration reform.

The Latino margin could have been even greater. Only 47% of the registered Latinos participated in the general election, 10% fewer than the white population.

Hispanics registered 7.4% of the vote in the most racially and ethnically diverse election in U.S. history. Blacks accounted for 12%.

In 2004, Latinos cast 6% of the vote, in an upward trend that started in 1988 with 3.6%.

And since the immigration surge has been around for two decades, the Latino vote is likely to produce an even larger share in 2012. It's estimated that two million new Latino voters will have come of age in time for the next presidential election. Every month, 50,000 Latinos who were born in the U.S., mostly to undocumented parents, will turn 18 and be eligible to vote.

Their folks won't be able to vote – not yet. But their kids will. And they'll vote Democratic.

In 2004, President George W. Bush won re-election with more than 44% of the Latino vote. Obama got 67% in 2008. He won over 75% of U.S. born Hispanics. He even made inroads with the Cuban-American community in Florida, a segment that's long been in the Republican fold.

Florida, Nevada, New Mexico and Colorado, all with large Latino populations, are now in the Democratic camp. Texas and Arizona likely will follow suit the next time around. California, with the largest numbers of Latinos, hasn't voted Republican since 1988.

While Republican tactics earned the party an anti-immigrant image, that issue wasn't the only reason Latinos went Democratic. However, it was and continues to be an important symbolic issue.

Latinos, a working class people, in the wake of the election care most about the economy. They responded to Obama's plan to avert foreclosures, to make health care and education more affordable, and to create jobs in infrastructure projects.

The Iraq War is also a concern of Hispanics. They are over-represented in the armed forces.

Republican leaders insist that Hispanics are more conservative than liberal, and thus have a "natural home" in the GOP. But they've failed to pay attention to the changing demographics.

Latinos now number 45.4 million, and account for 15% of the U.S. population. The Pew Hispanic Center projects that by the year 2050, that percentage will nearly double to 29%.

In a seven-year period, from 2000 to 2007, Latinos increased their numbers by 10 million. While six million of those were born in America – and thus are U.S. citizens – four million migrated from Latin America, the vast majority undocumented.

In 2008 an estimated 11.9 million unauthorized immigrants were living in the U.S. Eight million of those were in the work force. Nearly three-quarters of the children of those undocumented parents were born in the U.S.

Not all of the undocumented immigrants and their children are Hispanic, of course. Just the vast majority of them. More than three out of four are Latinos. Sixty per cent are from Mexico and another 11% are from Central America.

There now are 12.7 million Mexican immigrants living in the U.S., and they account for 32% of all immigrants. The second largest group of immigrants, Filipinos, registers only 5%.

No other country in the world has as many total immigrants as the U.S. has Mexican immigrants. About 11% of all who were born in Mexico are currently living in the U.S.

The numbers are staggering. But there is even more evidence of the browning of America on the horizon, and the political influence Latinos will wield in the future.

While there were an estimated 6.6 million undocumented Mexican immigrants in the U.S. in 2006, there were another 3.3 million "lawful permanent residents." These are the "green card" holders. They're not U.S. citizens, but most could be by 2012. A total of 2.7 million LPRs were deemed eligible to apply for citizenship in 2006.

In 2007, some 148,640 Mexican nationals were granted green cards. Of those nearly nine out of 10 were family-sponsored immigrants. Only about 8% was sponsored by employers.

In 2004, some 63,000 Mexicans became U.S. citizens. That year Mexico was the No. 1 country represented out of a total of 537,000 new citizens. It was estimated then that 11.3 million naturalized citizens were living in the U.S. with another eight million eligible to join the ranks.

New citizens are allowed to file petitions to legally bring kinfolk to the U.S., who later can apply to become "lawful permanent residents" with a future option of becoming naturalized U.S. citizens.

This enormous shift in demographics on the American continent is a relatively recent phenomenon. In 1970, there were only 760,000 Mexican-born immigrants in the U.S.

Back when Europe was sending boatloads of immigrants to the U.S., Mexicans were staying home. Irish immigrants represented more than one-third of the immigrant population from 1850 to 1870. Germans were about 30% of the foreign-born population from 1850 to 1900.

The total number of Mexican immigrants in the U.S. in 1890 was 78,000. As late as 1950, Mexicans accounted for only 4% of the foreign-born population.

But 30 years later, Mexico had the largest foreign-born population in the U.S. with 2.2 million immigrants, more than twice as many as second place Germany with 850,000.

The number of Mexican immigrants doubled from 1980 to 1990 and much more than doubled in the next decade. In 2008, the number had skyrocketed to 12.7 million. That's 17 times more than 1970.

In less than 40 years, the face of America has changed dramatically.

Mexican immigrants are still settling in the traditional destination states like California, which has a total of 4.3 million immigrants, including 1.9 million in the Los Angeles metropolitan area. Texas is in second place with 2.3 million. The other states with sizeable immigrant populations include, in descending order: Illinois, Arizona, Florida, Georgia, Colorado, North Carolina, Nevada and New York.

Those 10 states account for 83% of the total. Some 6.6 million Mexican immigrants reside in the top 15 metropolitan areas in the U.S.

But more and more Mexicans are spreading out into the Midwest and the South in search of jobs and better living conditions. The top five states in percentage growth in 2006 were South Dakota, Louisiana, Alaska, Ohio and New Jersey.

Most Mexicans, like other immigrants before them, first settle in communities where they have kinfolk. There they can find jobs, temporary housing, a common language and friendly advice in learning the ropes in a strange place. Later they move to other locations for greater opportunities.

They come to the U.S. from all 31 Mexican states. The leading states of origin have been those in the west-central part of the country, including Guanajuato, Jalisco, Michoacán, Nayarit and Zacatecas

But the latest waves of immigrants are disproportionately from the poorest states, Oaxaca and Chiapas, which also have the largest numbers of indigenous citizens. While the vast majority of Mexicans live in large cities and in major metropolitan areas, nearly half of the recent immigrants come from small towns and rural areas.

They aren't like other recent immigrant groups. They aren't even like their own people who entered the U.S. a quarter-century ago or even those who were born and grew up in America.

Of the total 11.5 million Mexican-born immigrants in the U.S. in 2006, nearly 28% entered the country since 2000; 34% in the 1990s; 20% in the 1980s; 11% in the 1970s, and just 6% before 1970.

A profile of a typical Mexican immigrant today points to a young man, with little education or job skills who grew up in the country or in a small village. His family was large and poor. He had kinfolk who had migrated to the U.S., and he was encouraged to join them.

While the median age is 35, many of the immigrants first came to America as teenagers. Most of them (57%) were male. Most of them (70%) were married. Most of them (61%) did not complete high school. Most of them (75%) couldn't speak English. Most of them (71%) worked at least one job.

They worked in construction, in manufacturing, in transportation, in maintenance and in services, mostly in restaurants. They earned an average of $23,000 a year. Their U.S.-born cousins made an average of $40,000 a year.

However, when the recession hit the U.S., the Mexican immigrants became the most vulnerable. The unemployment rate for foreign-born Hispanics went from 5% to 8% from fourth quarter 2007 to the fourth quarter in 2008. During the same period, the jobless rate for all people in the labor market increased from 4.6% to 6.6%.

Tough economic times also has had a major impact in the amount of money immigrants send to their families in Mexico. In 2008, remittances to Mexico totaled $23.8 billion, and that was 3.6% less than the year before. It's Mexico's second largest source of revenue after petroleum, and millions of families depend on the money to pay the bills and put food on the table.

The economic downturn, which limited job opportunities, along with greatly increased security measures, walls and Border Patrol surveillance on the U.S. border, have teamed up to sharply reduce the flow of immigrants from Mexico to the U.S.

In 2006-2007, a Mexican National Survey put the number of migrants leaving Mexico for the U.S. at more than one million. A similar survey in 2008-2009 listed only 636,000 leaving Mexico.

The Pew Hispanic Center survey noted that the Mexican-born population in the U.S. stood at 11.5 million in early 2009, and was not significantly different from the 11.6 million in 2008 or the 11.2 million in 2007.

Patterns of migration affect the statistical studies. Many immigrants come from Mexico to settle permanently. But large numbers move both ways across the U.S. border throughout the year, sometimes staying but a few months. Circular migration also tends to be seasonal, with larger northbound flows in spring and summer and larger southbound flows in the fall and winter.

The recession, however, is not sending many Mexicans back across the border. In February 2006, a Mexican survey estimated that 479,000 returned home. The next year, the number was 440,000, and last year it was 433,000.

The bottom line is that the number of Mexicans in America isn't going anywhere but up.

---

## Chapter Fourteen: IN THE U.S. of A.: Among the sources cited:

International Directory of Company Histories, Kimberly-Clark de Mexico, St. James Press, 2003.

Kevin Sieff, Brownsville Herald, "Hispanic Voice," Nov. 13, 2008.

Jill Lawrence, USA Today, "Hispanic vote grows, shifts to Democrats," Nov. 7, 2008.

Pew Hispanic Center, "Mexican immigrants in the Untied States," 2008.

Jeanne Batalova, Migration Policy Institute, "Mexican Immigrants in the U.S.," April 23, 2008.

U.S. Citizenship and Immigration Services, "USCIS citizenship and naturalization facts," Dec. 15, 2005.

Paul Wiseman, USA Today, "Migrants' families feel money pinch," Feb. 27, 2009.

A man on a "Border Pilgrimage" wears a t-shirt as a stark reminder of migrant deaths that occurred in the desert up to 2003. The number more than doubled to 5,000 over the next six years.

# Chapter Fifteen

## The Myths –1

✦

### 'Know-Nothings' legacy lives on

Critics of immigration reform frequently resort to two favorite challenges: "What is it that you don't understand about illegal?" And "why don't they just follow the rules like my great-grandparents did?"

The assumption, of course, is that grandpa was legal. He was, indeed, undocumented. Grandpa didn't need a visa because when he crossed the ocean from Germany and arrived at Ellis Island in New York, there wasn't any such thing.

There was no federal legislation restricting immigration in the country until the 1870s. In fact, immigration was encouraged – from Europe. Later, mental and physical health restrictions, along with moral standards, came into play. In 1875 convicts and prostitutes were banned and seven years later "idiots, lunatics and persons likely to become public charges" were turned away.

In 1882, the Chinese Exclusion Act was the first piece of legislation that restricted immigration on the basis of national origin.

Eleven million immigrants, mostly from European countries, arrived in the U.S. between 1870 and 1900. Less than 1% of them were rejected, mostly due to tuberculosis and other contagious diseases.

Each wave of immigrants had to survive deep discrimination and disdain from those who arrived before them. Prejudice grew out of fear of the unknown. Waves of Germans, who mostly spoke in their native tongue, and the Irish, whose thick brogues were difficult to understand, were two groups that provoked the "nativist" Americans.

Back in the 1850s, a secret society that was anti-immigrant, anti-Catholic and anti-Jewish rose into political prominence. They were called the "Know-

Nothings" for their secretive response. They held a national convention in Philadelphia in 1856 and nominated Millard Fillmore for president. Fillmore didn't fare so well, but the Know-Nothings' influence did spread across the country.

The movement that became the American Party elected 43 congressmen, five senators, along with eight governors and thousands of local government officials. The slavery issue soon occupied the day for the Know-Nothings and that split the party, with the anti-slavery adherents joining the newly emerging Republican Party and the pro-slavery supporters joining the Democratic Party.

The Know-Nothings era was over by 1859, but its prejudicial legacy has lived on well into the 21st century.

Today's "Know-Nothings" have become a formidable foe to millions of new immigrants of a different color. They fear those who don't speak their language, those who have a different culture. They fear the browning of America, the day when minorities will be majorities.

Their voice, while a minority in itself, is further amplified by today's new media messengers that are supplanting traditional, credible news sources. The bloggers now are free to spew whatever "wisdom" they have, often presented on a par with seasoned journalists. Right-wing radio commentators rile up their avid listeners with a mixture of half-truths and outright lies.

Cable television commentators like Lou Dobbs, Bill O'Reilly and Glenn Beck have especially taken on the immigration issue with both vitriol and by perpetuating myths. They've served up a steady diet of fear, anger and resentment, geared toward creating anti-immigrant hysteria.

While there is no end to the number of national issues that merit discussion – a faltering economy, a health-care crisis and the wars in Iraq and Afghanistan, for starters -- the topic of illegal immigration is foremost on their programs. Lou Dobbs, in particular, was obsessed about illegal aliens on 70% of his shows in 2007.

The commentators not only give credence to the common myths about crime and the costs of illegal immigration in social services and taxes, but they also promote ludicrous hearsay as truth. Among those urban legend myths are that Mexican immigrants are infecting Americans with leprosy and that there's a conspiracy for Mexico to take back the Southwest United States.

Respected opinion polls generally have a slight majority of Americans siding with the new immigrants, depending, of course, on the topic and questions asked. That favorable percentage is not reflected, however, in Internet blogs, letters to the editor, and congressional mailbags, which all run at least 10 to 1 against immigrants.

The loudest voice, as usual, belongs to the opposition.

Some have even taken to the Internet to rally forces to sign petitions to Congress that insist that: "the 12 to 20 million illegal aliens now here have to go home; there will be no new categories or programs through which they may re-enter; and that no child born in the U.S. shall be granted citizenship unless at least one parents is a U.S. citizen."

The myths that continue to feed on themselves are legion. At least a score or more of agencies, organizations and humanitarian groups, including widely diverse religions, have responded to the call to quell and dispel many of the myths. A sampling follows:

### Today's immigrants are different than those of 100 years ago.

*The percentage of the U.S. population that is foreign-born now stands at 11.5%; in the early 20$^{th}$ century it was approximately 15%.*

*Similar to accusations about today's immigrants, those of 100 years ago initially often settled in mono-ethnic neighborhoods, spoke their native languages and built up newspapers and businesses that catered to their fellow émigrés.*

*They also experienced the same types of discrimination that today's immigrants face, and integrated within American culture at a similar rate.*

**Sources: U.S. Council of Catholic Bishops' "Justice for Immigrants" campaign**

### Immigrants are overrunning our country and most are illegal.

*Of the 36 million immigrants in the U.S. today, two-thirds (24 million) are here legally, and half of those with legal status (12 million) are U.S. citizens.*

*There are an estimated 12 million undocumented immigrants in the U.S. Half*

*(6 million) of these people entered the country legally as tourists, students or temporary workers and became "undocumented" when their papers expired and they didn't leave the country.*

*Undocumented immigrants make up about 4% of the overall U.S. population, and only 2% have crossed the border outside of legal channels.*

**Source: 2009 Anti-Defamation League, Challenging Anti-immigrant Bias in the U.S.**

### Immigrants don't pay taxes and are a drain on the economy.

*All immigrants pay taxes. Even undocumented immigrants pay sales taxes and real estate taxes, either directly as homeowners or indirectly through rent.*

*The Social Security Administration estimates that three-quarters of undocumented immigrants contribute payroll taxes, including $6 to $7 billion in Social Security taxes that will never benefit them.*

*Approximately 26 million immigrants currently residing in the U.S. arrived after the age of 18 and are in prime working age. They represent roughly $2.8*

*trillion to U.S. taxpayers who receive the benefit of their labor without the cost of their education.*
**Sources: Lutheran Immigration and Refugee Service, Immigration Myths and Facts**

## Immigrants take jobs away from Americans

*Immigration has a positive effect on the American economy. Immigrants have different skills, which allows higher skilled native workers to increase productivity and thus increase their incomes.*

*The President's Council on Economic Advisors in 2007 estimated the annual wage gain due to immigration for U.S. workers was more than $30 billion per year.*

*The CEA acknowledged that an increase in immigrant workers was likely to have some negative impact on the wages of low-skilled native workers, but they found the impact to be relatively small, and concluded that reducing immigration "would be a poorly-targeted and inefficient way top assist low-wage Americans."*
**Sources: American Civil Liberties Union, National Research Council, Council of Economic Advisors**

## U.S. spends billions on welfare for undocumented immigrants

*Undocumented immigrants are not eligible to receive any "welfare" benefits and even legal immigrants are severely restricted in the benefits they can receive.*

*Legal permanent residents must pay into the Social Security and Medicare systems for approximately 10 years before they are eligible to receive benefits when they retire.*

*Less than 1% of households headed by undocumented immigrants received assistance for needy families in 2007, compared to 5% of households headed by native-born U.S. citizens.*
**Sources: Ending the Immigration Spin, Congressional Research Service, Urban Institute**

## Undocumented immigrants are more likely to commit crimes

*Both undocumented and legal immigrants are significantly less likely to commit crimes than U.S. citizens.*

*A 2007 study showed that the male incarceration rate for the native-born (3.5%) was five times higher than the rate for immigrants (0.7%).*

*Newly arrived immigrants are especially unlikely to be involved in crime, and teenage immigrants are less likely to be involved in delinquent behavior, such as violence and drug use.*
**Sources: University of California-Irvine, Federal Reserve Bank of Chicago, Anti-Defamation League**

## Immigrants don't want to assimilate into U.S. society

*Immigrants learn English and climb the socioeconomic ladder over time, and their children and grandchildren make even greater strides.*

*A 2007 study showed that among adult first generation Latinos, just 23% say they can carry on a conversation in English very well. That rises sharply to 88% among the second generation of adults, and to 94% among third generations.*

*Many immigrants seek citizenship despite difficult requirements and long delays. In 2007 the Department of Homeland Security received 1.4 million citizenship applications, and in recent years the number of new citizens has risen to the highest level in 25 years.*

**Sources: Pew Hispanic Center, Russell Sage Foundation, Rand Corporation,**

## Immigrants send all their money to their home countries

*More than half of the immigrants send money to their families back home. Remittances are the biggest sources of foreign currency for most Latin American countries, surpassing any amount of foreign aid sent by the U.S.*

*However, they do spend money in the U.S., too. In addition to paying taxes and Social Security, immigrants spend money on goods and services. A study showed that they become net economic contributors after 10 years in the U.S.*

*In addition to increased spending, immigrants contribute about $162 billion in tax revenue to U.S. federal, state and local governments.*

**Sources: Cato Institute, Inter-American Development Bank,   American Civil Liberties Union**

## The war on terrorism is linked illegal immigration

*No security analyst has said that tougher restrictions on immigration will prevent a terrorist attack. All of the 9/11 terrorists were in the U.S. legally. Since 9/11 the myriad of measures targeting thousands of immigrants in the name of national security have netted no terrorism prosecutions. One study of 400 terrorists showed that only 6% had entered the country illegally.*

*Many experts now believe that unfairly targeting immigrants causes the U.S. to be less safe by making immigrants afraid to contact police with information about crimes.*

**Sources: Anti-Defamation League, Challenging Anti-Immigrant Bias in the U.S.**

## Border enforcement is the best solution to illegal immigration

*Policies geared only toward sealing the border or deporting the undocumented without reforming the immigration system would cost the U.S. hundreds of billions of dollars and have a devastating effect on vast swaths of the U.S. economy.*

*A 2005 study estimates that it would cost up to $230 billion over five years to deport all undocumented immigrants from the U.S. If that were to be done, the U.S. labor force would have a shortfall of nearly 2.5 million less-skilled workers.*

*In 2006 Congress provided $3 billion for 700 miles of fencing stretching from California to Texas, designed to prevent illegal immigration from Mexico. The number of Border Patrol agents was doubled and the agency's budget was increased 10 times. Yet the number of undocumented immigrants in the U.S. increased from 8 million in 2000 to 12 million in 2009.*

**Sources: Center for American Progress, Pew Hispanic Center, Ant-Defamation League**

# Chapter Fifteen

## *The Myths – 2*

✦

### *Five million on waiting list to get U.S. visas*

Send 'em all back to wherever they came from! And don't let 'em cut in line!

The simplistic response to a highly complex problem has become the familiar cry of the modern day "Know-Nothings." It begs for a closer examination.

There are 12 million undocumented immigrants living in the U.S. While they have come from all over the world, the majority are Mexicans. Include the Latinos from Central America and the number of those speaking Spanish takes a commanding lead.

It's a daunting task. How do you round up 12 million people who mostly live in the shadows and ship them back to their home countries? If that were even possible, if not desirable, the costs would be astronomical. One estimate for the mass deportation put the price tag at $250 billion.

And that's not all. The U.S. economy would go from recession to depression overnight with the loss of more than 2.5 million workers in areas critical to consumers. Who would pick the tomatoes? Who would milk the cows? Who would slaughter the livestock? Who would put on roofs and landscape yards? Who would clean offices and hotel rooms, and who would take care of the kids? A recent film, "*A Day without a Mexican*," tells a convincing tale of a California "what if."

Now, most of these "illegal aliens" didn't just arrive in the U.S. Several million of them have been around for 25 years or more. Many own houses; some own businesses. Most have been paying taxes for years. They've also contributed to Social Security, even though they'll never be able to cash in on the retirement benefits. Their kids and their grandkids were born in the U.S.A. and thus are citizens. In most cases, one of the spouses is legal.

There are now five million people around the world on the waiting list to get into the U.S.

The conundrum has been caused, not by the immigrants themselves but by Congressional inaction on immigration reform, by businesses relishing and recruiting low-cost labor, and by spotty enforcement of immigration laws.

For more than two decades, the federal government hasn't been able to make up its mind whether illegal immigration is good or bad for the country. The U.S. has put up barriers at the border but often they've been deliberately surmountable. It became a challenge. If a Mexican could make it across, he was rewarded with a job. And if he didn't screw up, he had a lifetime pass for himself and his family.

At first, it was a matter of thousands who crossed the frontier and quickly assimilated into Latino communities in California, Texas and Arizona. Then came the migrant surges caused by worsening economic conditions in Mexico in the 1980s. Then there was the NAFTA effect that cost two million agricultural jobs in the 1990s. Suddenly there were millions of Mexicans without legal documents working base-tier jobs, often well below minimum wage, and they were spread throughout the U.S.

The wake-up call, of course, was 9/11. All at once national security was at the forefront of an immigration issue that had gotten out of control. There were holes in the fences that needed to be plugged, and in the name of terrorism, the national sentiment, often irrationally, turned against the immigrants.

The immediate response of many Americans was: "Build the wall and deport 'em all!"

So 700 miles of the Great Wall of Mexico were built at a cost of a couple billion dollars, the U.S. Border Patrol was beefed up and high-tech surveillance equipment was installed to cover the gaps in the 2,000-mile border.

And still they came, many of them teenage boys with a fourth grade education, with no opportunities and facing a bleak future. They trekked the dangerous migrant trails across mountains and deserts, defying death just to get any job in the United States.

By 2006, more than 10% of those born in Mexico were living in the U.S. At least half of them were illegal.

In a show to prove to the American public that the government was serious about controlling illegal immigration, the U.S. Immigration and Customs Enforcement agency (ICE) conducted a series of controlled workplace raids. A few thousand Latinos were deported at an enormous cost to their families, to their communities, to the companies that employed them and to the taxpayers who had to pay the bills.

Many Americans had misgivings about the Gestapo enforcement tactics that demonized and criminalized an impoverished and semi-illiterate workforce. They sympathized with the immigrants who already had been used and abused by their employers. Besides, no one was standing in line to get a job at the slaughterhouses, where many of the raids occurred.

The raids suddenly came to a halt. The public and the politicians didn't have the stomach to continue picking on the poor, even if they were labeled illegal aliens.

So, if there was little support for deporting a few thousand newcomers, how is the U.S. going to round up and ship out millions of Mexicans, many of whom have been an integral part of their communities for a couple of decades?

There are no easy answers in the contentious immigration issue that has festered for more than a quarter-century.

The immigration laws and procedures are so complex that few can wade through the bureaucratic maize without an attorney who specializes in the field. The quotas and the categories and the preferences are constantly shifting, and the backlogs and waiting lists are constantly growing.

The numbers are alarming. Actually, they're way out of control. More than five million people are waiting for family visas. That's 20 times the number that can be legally issued each year. Critics assert that the current system is unfair to both applicants and their sponsors. Besides, it's a big waste of government resources.

There also is evidence that maintaining such a large waiting list of "pending" applications creates an incentive, or at least rationalization, for illegal immigration.

Moreover, it seems like a cruel joke to tell applicants that they qualify for a green card, take their application fees, and then tell them it will be years before they can claim it.

Mission Mexico has the largest consular operation in the world. It handles one million legal border crossings each day. It represents one million American citizens who are Mexican residents and more than 12 million Americans who visit Mexico for business or tourism each year.

Besides those services to American citizens, in 2007 it processed Mexican requests for 1.5 million non-immigrant visas to the U.S. for visitors, students and temporary workers. By the year 2011, that number is expected to exceed 2.5 million.

On the average, consular officers in Mission Mexico interview more than 25,000 non-immigrant visa applicants each week.

Every day, as many as 2,000 Mexicans wait patiently for interviews at the U.S. Embassy in Mexico City, hoping to obtain a visa to visit the United

States. Most, especially the poor, are unsuccessful. Meanwhile, every day thousands of Mexicans cross the U.S. border by *coyote*.

It's not easy to get a visa just to visit the United States. Mexicans need a portfolio of documents that includes proof of financial support, and evidence that the visit is temporary. They also have to demonstrate strong ties to Mexico that would compel them to return. That's the clause that trips up the poor.

Applicants must fill out an I-94 arrival/departure form and submit to a personal interview. The visa, if approved, will get them to a port of entry. There the U.S. customs officer determines whether the visitor is permitted to enter the U.S. and how long he can stay.

There's a much easier way to be able to visit the U.S. Just be a citizen of one of 27 countries that belong to the Visa Waiver Program. Citizens of countries that include the likes of Brunei, Singapore and Slovenia don't need a visa. Most of the European countries are also exempt for 90-day stays.

The Visa Waiver Program was established in 1986 to promote tourism and better relations with U.S. allies. More Mexicans visit the U.S. than any other country. And vice versa. Americans don't need a visa to visit Mexico. But it's not reciprocal.

Mexico is at the top of the list in most categories dealing with U.S. immigration. About 80% of the H2 visas (temporary workers) processed throughout the world are issued in Mexico, although that number was only 150,000 in 2007. It leads in both categories of non-immigrant admissions.

If you want to reside and work legally in the U.S., you'll need a "green card." That's shorthand for "legal permanent resident." In 2008, more than one million people became LPRs. About 17% of them were born in Mexico.

There's a complex pecking order for LPR applications. If you are a U.S. citizen, you can apply on a family-based first preference for your unmarried sons and daughters. There are four other categories with set quotas.

However, if you have a graduate degree in computer science, you can go to the head of the line. Employment-based preferences for "aliens with extraordinary ability" are courted by both the U.S. and its high-tech industries.

The quota for professionals and college-educated immigrants (H1B visas) recently was increased from 115,000 to 195,000 annually. Over a three-year period, the Third World "brain drain" now contributes nearly 600,000 highly skilled workers to the U.S. economy.

And they don't have to wait long for that visa. If the employer puts up an extra $1,000, the immigrant will have the H1B visa expressed to him within 15 days.

Mexicans don't figure heavily in that category. Researchers from India dominate the field with 38% of the total H1B visas issued in 2008. Mexico had 4%.

A million Mexicans have to compete for the 10,000 unskilled worker visas that are issued worldwide each year.

That's why there are 12 million undocumented immigrants working menial jobs for next to nothing and living in the shadows of the U.S.

---

## Chapter Fifteen: THE MYTHS: Among the sources cited:

Jessica Vaughan, Center for Immigration Studies,  "Five million waiting on family visas," May 19, 2009.

U.S. Embassy, Consular Affairs, "Mexico at a Glance," September 2008.

James D. Eiss,  immigration attorney; "Immigrant visa preferences," Sept. 29, 2008.

Randall Monger, U.S. Dept. of Homeland Security, "Non-immigrant admissions to the U.S.," 2008.

U.S. Dept. of State, Bureau of Consular Affairs, "Visa Bulletin," September 2009.

Fear and Loathing in Prime Time,  "Immigration myths and cable news," 2007.

Five Catholic bishops, from Ciudad Juárez, El Paso, San Antonio, Laredo and Las Cruces, concelebrated mass on "El Dia de Los Muertos" in 2003 on both sides of the border fence as Anapra, NM, in memory of the migrants who died trying to get to the U.S.

# Chapter Sixteen

## *The Solution – 1*

✦

### *Congressional divide stymies real reform*

○ ○ ○ ○ ○ ○ ○ ○ ○ ○ ○ ○ ○ ○ ○ ○ ○ ○ ○ ○ ○ ○ ○ ○ ○ ○ ○ ○ ○ ○ ○ ○ ○ ○ ○

*"The new immigrants are good for America. They are revitalizing our cities, building our new economy. They are energizing our culture and broadening our vision of the world.*

*"America has constantly drawn strength and spirit from wave after wave of immigrants. They have proved to be the most restless, the most adventurous, the most innovative, most industrious of people.*

*"They are renewing our basic values and reminding us all of what it truly means to be an American."*

**--President Bill Clinton, Commencement address at Portland State University, June 13, 1998.**

Back in the spring of 2005 it appeared that the U.S. Congress would finally get serious about long-overdue immigration legislation.

There was an air of urgency throughout the nation. The number of illegal aliens was soaring. There were an estimated 11.1 million unauthorized immigrants in the U.S., and 4.4 million of those had arrived since the year 2000. They were coming at a rate of 850,000 a year, and that five-year period accounted for more than 40% of the total.

During that time, the number of unauthorized Mexicans increased by 1.5 million, from 4.7 million to 6.2 million. Illegal immigrants from Central America increased by 465,000 to 1.4 million. Together, undocumented Latinos accounted for 8.7 million, or 78% of the 11.1 million total in 2005.

The southern border with Mexico was especially porous. The War on Terrorism was well underway in the Persian Gulf and elsewhere and the Department of Homeland Security was feeling insecure about the unimpeded crossings along the Rio Grande and the desert southwest.

That year saw the introduction of two pieces of legislation, vastly opposite in philosophy and practice. Few held out hope for any Congressional compromise.

The Senate version focused on what to do with undocumented immigrants already in the country; the House version focused on getting them out and keeping them out.

While party lines were occasionally crossed, the stalemate in the end essentially pitted Democrats against Republicans.

Rep. James Sensenbrenner of Wisconsin, the House Judiciary chairman, along with Homeland Security chairman Peter King of New York, co-sponsored the "Border Protection, Antiterrorism and Illegal Immigrant Control Act of 2005." In legislative shorthand it was known as H.R. 4437.

Sensenbrenner, a conservative Republican in office since 1979, had a long history of supporting anti-immigrant legislation. He became the point man and the center of the storm over H.R. 4437. The bill passed the House on a 239-182 vote on Dec. 16, 2005.

It made "unlawful presence" a crime and document fraud an aggravated felony. It threatened loss of federal funding for states and local governments that didn't enforce federal immigration laws. It eliminated the diversity visa lottery program that allows 50,000 immigrants each year to permanently reside in the U.S. It extended detention and deportation measures for illegal aliens. It increased worksite enforcement penalties and insisted on employer verification of worker status.

One of the most controversial measures threatened "Good Samaritans" with criminal penalties and five years in prison for knowingly assisting an undocumented immigrant. This could include church personnel who provide shelter or other basic needs.

Cardinal Roger Mahoney of the Los Angeles Catholic Archdiocese publicly stated the church would continue to aid immigrants and defy that sanction.

While H.R. 4437 never became law, many of its border security proposals did. The 700 miles of new fencing along the Mexican border was later approved along with high-tech surveillance equipment. A study of the possibility of a fence along the Canadian border, however, was stalled.

The Senate bill, co-sponsored by Sen. Edward Kennedy, a Massachusetts Democrat, and Sen. John McCain, an Arizona Republican, took a comprehensive approach toward immigration reform.

It included border security as well as legalization and guest worker programs. It was called "Secure America and Orderly Immigration Act," (S. 1033). Some labeled it the "McKennedy Bill." The U.S. Senate voted 62-36 on May 25, 2006, in favor. Two years later, in the midst of the presidential campaign, Sen. McCain, in a move to appease conservatives, said that he couldn't support his own bill.

The amended measure called for 370 miles of fencing and more than doubling the U.S. Border Patrol numbers. It allowed illegal immigrants who had been in the U.S. for five years or more to remain, on a track to become legal permanent residents and eventually citizens after paying fines and fees. It required illegal immigrants with two to five years in the U.S. to return to their country and file an application to return.

It also created a guest worker program for an estimated 1.5 million farm workers, along with creating 200,000 new temporary guest worker visas. The H-1B visas for skilled workers were increased from 65,000 to 115,000 annually.

The Senate bill fomented charges of "amnesty," reflecting on that failed policy of the Reagan Administration to control illegal immigration. Republicans lined up to oppose any concessions for illegal aliens, even though President George W. Bush had endorsed many of the provisions.

There were other versions and attempts at honing a compromise bill that might have had a chance to make it through Congress before the presidential campaign entered the home stretch. But time ran out, and the measures died before they even came up for a vote.

In early 2007, Kennedy and McCain girded for a new go-around. A bill, which was drafted in consultation with the White House, largely mirrored the one the two senators co-sponsored two years earlier.

Congressional leaders, at loggerheads, had put immigration on a fast track, hoping to find an acceptable solution before the 2008 presidential campaign consumed the nation's political energy.

There were several versions presented before the Senate settled on "The Comprehensive Immigration Reform Act of 2007" (S. 1348). The bill's sole sponsor was Majority Leader Harry Reid, although it was put together by Kennedy and McCain, with input from President Bush and support from the "Gang of 12" in the Senate. The bill was portrayed as a compromise between providing a path to citizenship for illegal immigrants and increased border enforcement. However, it was doomed by criticism from both sides of the aisle.

It never made it to the floor. On June 7, 2007, three Senate votes on cloture (a move to end discussion) failed and the bill was declared dead.

However, at the urging of President Bush, a revised bill was brought back 18 days later as S. 1639. It, too, died of cloture on June 26.

That bill contained a number of new provisions, some of which likely will be resurrected once the 111th U.S. Congress again confronts the issue. Among the changes:

-- It would create a new class of visa, the "Z Visa," that would be given to everyone who was living without a valid visa in the U.S. on Jan. 1, 2008. It would make them legal and eligible for a Social Security number. After eight years, they would be eligible for a "green card" after paying a fine and back taxes. Five years later, they could start the process of becoming a U.S. citizen.

-- Another new category of visa, the "Y Visa," would let temporary guest workers stay in the country for two years, after which they would have to return home. The original bill allowed 400,000 people a year in the program.

-- It would increase enforcement along the U.S.-Mexico border, upping the number of Border Patrol agents to 20,000 and adding another 370 miles of fencing.

-- It would create a new program, the "Employment Eligibility Verification System," a central database to hold immigrant-status information on all workers living in the U.S.

-- It would contain provisions for "The Dream Act," a bill that has been introduced unsuccessfully several times in the House and Senate. It provides a path to citizenship for illegal immigrant minors who either go to college or serve in the U.S. military.

The revised Comprehensive Immigration Reform Act of 2007 (S. 1639) is not without its harsh critics, both on the right and on the left. Conservatives reject providing a path to citizenship for illegal immigrants. Liberals criticize the provisions limiting family reunification visas. Labor unions attack some aspects of the guest worker program and high-tech industries don't like scrapping the employer-sponsored "green card" applications.

The American public also is deeply divided about the solution to the immigration issue. But they do want a resolve to the dilemma.

Some want it more than others. While overall few Americans rate immigration reform as the most important problem now facing the country, it's a different story in Phoenix where 55% of those polled said it was a "very big" problem. Other communities with growing immigrant populations, like Las Vegas and Raleigh-Durham, also see it as a priority both for their community and the country.

In the spring of 2006, the Pew Hispanic Center surveyed and compiled the results of 12 distinct opinion polls, ranging from Fox News to Gallup to

Bloomberg to Newsweek. The respected research center also included its own findings on a number of immigration-related issues.

Among the combined conclusions:

-- The public is evenly divided over whether increased immigration is good or bad for the country.

-- Most Americans see illegal immigration as a serious problem.

-- Most Americans believe that illegal immigrants are taking jobs that Americans do not want.

-- Most Americans favor measures that would allow illegal immigrants to remain in the U.S. either as permanent residents and eventual citizens or as temporary workers.

-- Most Americans expressed greater confidence in Democrats on immigration issues than Republicans.

Opinion polls, of course, fluctuate with the times, locations and extenuating circumstances. In 2006, immigration issues were in fifth place in the national psyche, trailing health care, terrorism and crime. On local levels, they sometimes didn't beat out traffic congestion and jobs availability.

In 2009, health care reform and the troubled economy greatly outdistanced immigration issues.

President Barack Obama, attending a North American summit with the leaders of Mexico and Canada in August 2009, said his administration would pursue a comprehensive overhaul of the U.S. immigration system. But he added that no action on legislation was expected until 2010.

He cited more pressing issues, such as health-care reform, energy legislation and financial regulatory changes.

Immigration reform would have to wait its turn.

# Chapter Sixteen

## *The Solution –2*

✦

### *Immigration reform at heart of U.S. values*

○ ○ ○ ○ ○ ○ ○ ○ ○ ○ ○ ○ ○ ○ ○ ○ ○ ○ ○ ○ ○ ○ ○ ○ ○ ○ ○ ○ ○ ○ ○ ○ ○ ○ ○ ○

*"America has nothing to fear from today's immigrants. They have come here for the same reason that families have always come here – for the hope that in America they could build a better life for themselves and their families.*

*"Like the wave of immigrants that came before them and the Hispanic Americans whose families have been here for generations, the recent arrival of Latino immigrants will only enrich our country."*

**--Barack Obama, speech to National Association of Latino Officials, June 28, 2008.**

"Comprehensive immigration reform" means different things to different people. Most everyone concedes that the system is broken, and piecemeal legislation won't fix it. Most everyone would agree that the solution should be "comprehensive."

But they also realize that "the devil is in the details."

Republican President George W. Bush favored a "comprehensive" approach. So does Democrat President Barack Obama. Neither plan has received a warm reception by their partisans, to say nothing about their political foes.

There is no easy answer to illegal immigration in the age of global economics. Products and jobs freely flow throughout the world without regard to national boundaries. Multi-national corporations are in a race to the bottom to find the cheapest work force to enhance their bottom lines.

The goods are exported. But the workers are left behind, and fences are constructed to keep them confined.

Two million Mexican corn farmers lost their livelihoods and their land to NAFTA's unfair trade policies over the past decade. They couldn't compete with the highly efficient and heavily subsidized U.S. corporate farms. One result was that most of the tortillas now consumed in Mexico are made with corn imported from the U.S.

Another result is that most of those once self-sufficient Mexican farmers now are "illegal aliens," laboring in the U.S. corn belt, in the fertile fields of California or dairy farms in Wisconsin. Undocumented immigrants now account for four out of every 10 agriculture jobs in "America's Dairyland."

If they had their druthers, they'd prefer to be farming and living in the land of their ancestors, rather than be estranged from their families during the cold Wisconsin winters. If they had a choice, they'd prefer to be legal rather than be living in the shadows, constantly on alert for the "migras."

So, who's to blame for the millions of migrants who have crossed mountains, rivers and perilous deserts in a desperate attempt to find a job, any job, to feed their families?

Is it the victims themselves who seek only work? Is it the American businesses that recruit bargain-wage employees? Is it the U.S. politicians who have stalled any meaningful immigration reform for more than a generation? Is it the corrupt Mexican government that has failed to create jobs at home for its rapidly growing population?

The questions lead to the crux of the solution.

There's plenty of blame to go around, of course. But up until now, the "illegal alien" mostly has been cited for his own plight. The U.S. enforcement policies, fences, border patrols, raids, detentions and deportations are all directed at punishing the victim.

However, almost all organized religions and humanitarian groups come down on the side of the migrant. Most point to numerous biblical and other religious statements to support fair play and justice for the sojourners in a foreign land.

> *"The strangers who sojourn with you shall be to you as the natives among you, and you shall love them as yourself; for you were strangers in the land of Egypt."*
>
> **--The Hebrew Bible, Leviticus 19:33-34.**

*"I was a stranger and you welcomed me.... What you do for the least of my brethren, you do unto me."*

**--The New Testament, Matthew 25:35, 40-41.**

*"Serve God and do good to orphans, those in need, neighbors who are near, neighbors who are strangers; the companion by your side, the wayfarer that you meet."*

**–The Qur'an, 4:36**

*"The guest is a representative of God."*

**--The Hindu Taltirlya Upanishad, 1.11.2**

While the religions pontificate on high, that welcoming message rarely resounds from the pulpits or the pews. And it's lost entirely on many once they exit the doors of the temple, mosque, church and synagogue. The faithful don't always practice what they've been preached.

Back in 2004, more than 300 faith-based groups from throughout the U.S. endorsed legislation that would lead to comprehensive immigration reform. They called for a policy that would uphold the human dignity of each person made in the image of God.

Before federal legislation was introduced, they proposed guidelines that included:

-- Reforms in our family-based immigration system to significantly reduce waiting times for separated families who now wait years to be reunited.

-- An opportunity for immigrants already contributing to this country to regularize their status upon satisfaction of reasonable criteria and pursue an option to become lawful permanent residents and eventually U.S. citizens.

-- The creation of legal avenues for workers and their families who wish to migrate to the U.S. to work in an orderly manner with their rights protected.

-- Border protection policies that are consistent with humanitarian values and with the need to treat all individuals with respect, while allowing authorities to pursue the task of implementing American immigration policy.

Among the 300 national organizations that signed on in support of comprehensive immigration reform, consistent with the values of their diverse faith traditions, are:

U.S. Conference of Catholic Bishops; Lutheran Immigration and Refugee Service; Presbyterian Church USA; Episcopal Church USA; United Methodist Church general board; American Baptist Churches USA; Unitarian Universalist Association; American Jewish Congress; Islamic Circle of North America; Hindu American Foundation, and Gamaliel National Clergy Caucus.

The U.S. Catholic hierarchy, through its "Justice for Immigrants" campaign, especially has been supportive of the new immigrants. Most of them, the vast majority of Latinos, are Roman Catholics who are expected to become a dominant force in the U.S. Catholic Church in coming decades. Latinos make up one-third of today's Catholics. Among those Catholics under 30 years old, 60% are Latinos.

The U.S. bishops, in accord with their Mexican counterparts, have proposed five basic principles to guide policymakers in creating immigration reform legislation:

**-- Persons have the right to find opportunities in their homeland.** All persons have the right to find in their own countries the economic, political and social opportunities to live in dignity and achieve a full life through the use of their God-given gifts. Work that provides a just, living wage is a basic human need.

**-- Persons have the right to migrate to support themselves and their families.** When persons cannot find employment in their country of origin to support themselves and their families, they have a right to find work elsewhere in order to survive. Sovereign nations should provide ways to accommodate this right.

**-- Sovereign nations have a right to control their borders.** The Church recognizes the right of sovereign nations to control their territories but rejects such control when it is exerted merely for the purpose of acquiring additional wealth. More powerful economic nations, which have the ability to protect and feed their residents, have a stronger obligation to accommodate migration flows.

**-- Refugees and asylum seekers should be afforded protection.** Those who flee wars and persecution should be protected by the global community. This requires, at a minimum, that migrants have a right to claim refugee status without incarceration and to have their claims fully considered by a competent authority.

**-- The human dignity and human rights of undocumented migrants should be respected.** Regardless of their legal status, migrants, like all persons, possess inherent human dignity that should be respected. Often they are subject to punitive laws and harsh treatment from enforcement officers from both receiving and transit countries. Government policies that respect the basic human rights of the undocumented are necessary.

Some Catholic bishops have been quite outspoken in defense of undocumented migrants. Cardinal Roger Mahoney of Los Angeles, California, whose archdiocese of five million is nearly half Latino, has publicly criticized the harsh enforcement immigration laws.

Over on the East Coast, Bishop Thomas Wenski of Orlando, Florida, recently joined the fray. "The so-called illegals are not so because they wish to defy the law, but because the law does not provide them with any channels to regularize their status in our country – which needs their labor," he said. "They are not breaking the law; the law is breaking them."

So, if they're not breaking the law, and their labor is needed and is sought to shore up the U.S. economy, the real solution to the immigration quandary is not to prosecute migrants but rather to welcome them and make them legal.

America did welcome more than nine million immigrants without documents of any kind over a 10-year period a century ago. They came from Europe by the boatload, were processed at Ellis Island, and joined their kinfolk in enclaves throughout the U.S., sticking together and speaking their native languages.

The foreign-born in 1910 represented 15% of the total population. They, too, experienced discrimination, but they took their place at the bottom of the ladder and a generation later they were mostly assimilated in the American fabric of society.

Today's foreign-born, while much larger in numbers, represents 11.5% of the total U.S. population.

Many people of European descent who were born in the U.S. decry today's surge of immigrants, especially those of other races from developing countries. About half of them have come from Latin American nations and one-third from Asia. They're especially irate about the undocumented, and often attempt to relate their grandparents' experiences to today's immigrant.

Why can't they come to the U.S. legally like their ancestors did, is the oft-repeated cry. The easy response is they can't because the U.S. won't issue them a visa. And, by the way, their great-grandparents didn't have a visa either.

There's another critical difference between the immigrants of old and those of today. The U.S. had nothing to do with those Europeans fleeing their homelands. America didn't cause the conditions that bought millions of Germans and Irish to U.S. shores.

However, that's not the case with today's Mexican migrants. The U.S. government, along with its First World allies, has been directly involved in trade, economic and political issues that have forced the migration of millions of Hispanics. And since the U.S. bears more than a little of the blame, it's morally obligated to come up with a just solution.

The United States orchestrated the North American Free Trade Agreement that over the last 15 years has proven to be an unmitigated disaster for Mexico's agriculture industry and has impoverished half of its population. The trickle-up economics has created lots of millionaires and millions of desperate poor.

NAFTA needs to be renegotiated to make free trade fair. If Mexico can't subsidize its corn farmers, the U.S. can't either.

Over the years, the U.S. has invested billions of dollars in self-serving projects in Mexico. The current $1.6 billion "Mérida Initiative" sounds generous at first glance. It's aimed to curb the drug wars, but it's also about U.S. security as well as the country's addiction to illicit narcotics. Besides, almost all the money is to be spent with U.S. contractors.

That keeps jobs in the U.S., but it doesn't do anything for Mexico's economy. The drug trade and the migrant exodus both are related to poverty. The pay differential between a U.S. and a Mexican worker is at least $10 to $1, and in some locations often much greater. If the U.S. is serious about slowing the flow of undocumented immigrants, it'll have to do more than build taller walls.

Instead of sending a billion dollars in armaments to bolster the Mexican military, the U.S. would get a better return on its money by investing in infrastructure that'll produce jobs. Instead of spending billions and billions attempting to ferret out and deport illegal aliens, the U.S. would be better served by putting that money to use at the source.

There are no easy solutions, of course, to the immigration dilemma.

No, the U.S. won't round up and ship out 12 million illegal aliens. Even if it could be done, it would cost at least $250 billion and result in the loss of at least 5% of the total U.S. labor force. Undocumented workers now represent 25% of all drywall installers, meat and poultry workers, ground maintenance workers and construction laborers. The U.S. economy would grind to a halt.

Besides, the immigrants are filling holes in the job market as more educated Americans take higher-paying and higher-skilled jobs.

Since many undocumented immigrants have lived and worked in the U.S. for a decade or more, they're likely to have several U.S.-born citizens among their children. The Pew Hispanic Center in 2005 estimated there were 3.1 million children born in the U.S. of undocumented parents. Should the U.S. have a policy of splitting up families, or should it amend the U.S. Constitution to take away their kids citizenship?

Should the U.S. tell José that he has to return to Mexico and stay there, taking his place in line for 10 years or more to get a visa to return to the U.S. to see his kids? He's not likely to do so.

Should all immigrants be forced to pay stiff fines for living and working in the U.S. without proper papers? If there's no crime, there's no call for punishment.

The lesson for legislators is not to sell out to emotional or racial bias to make unfair laws that will neither be respected nor enforced.

Comprehensive immigration reform is an urgent priority that needs to be addressed by the 111th U.S. Congress. The details must be hammered out within the guidelines of a fairness doctrine that includes at least seven principles:

-- **Temporary worker program:** Provides a path to permanent residency, enables family unity, offers job portability and labor protections, and protects domestic workers.

-- **Broad-based legalization:** A program that provides an opportunity for permanent residency. "Earned" legalization should be achievable and independently verifiable.

-- **Family-based immigration reform:** Provisions which reduce backlogs in the 2A visa category, immediate family of legal permanent residents, without affecting other preference categories.

-- **Smart and humane enforcement:** Border and interior enforcement that is targeted, proportional and humane, focusing on the most dangerous, and fairly enforcing immigration laws.

-- **Detention reform:** Provisions amending mandatory detention laws, expanding alternatives to detention, offering parole to families, codifying and improving detention standards and increasing oversight of detention facilities.

-- **Restoration of due process protections:** Provisions restoring judicial discretion in deportation proceedings.

-- **Addressing root causes of migration:** An examination of root causes of migration, such as lack of development in sending countries, and a plan to seek long-term solutions.

The roots of migration are at the core of the quandary. Few immigration critics ever pause to ponder why so many Latinos are leaving their homes, their families, their comfort zones to be treated so badly in the U.S. The vast majority isn't following the American Dream. They're just trying to survive.

They've become pawns in the game of global economics.

National security was said to be the driving force to control immigration in the wake of 9-11. The U.S. built a multi-billion-dollar wall of shame on its southern frontier, high-tech surveillance instruments were installed and the Border Patrol was greatly bolstered. The number of illegal crossings did decline a bit, in large part due to a faltering U.S. economy.

But the U.S. still didn't have any idea who or where or what 12 million undocumented immigrants were doing.

If they were allowed to become legal residents, they'd be accounted for. If they submitted to interviews and fingerprinting, if their status and numbers were realistically controlled and if they were given visas, national security would be much enhanced.

Comprehensive immigration reform is needed to take the unregulated, illegal and disorderly flow of unscreened and unauthorized workers and replace it with a legal, orderly, limited flow of vetted and authorized workers.

The largest potential supply, and the greatest need for workers in the U.S. are, by far, in the low-skill job categories. Yet only 5,000 visas are available per year for such permanent workers. This dichotomy is directly related to illegal immigration. And that has led to abuses in the workplace.

Another major factor driving Hispanic migration is family unity, also one of America's most cherished values. Restrictive laws and bureaucratic delays are to blame for lengthy separations of spouses and children. For example, a wife, husband or child of a U.S. Lawful Permanent Resident has to wait more than five years for a visa to enter the U.S.

There's no question but that immigration reform is fraught with complexities, as well as political posturing, at every turn. If it were easy, the U.S. Congress would have settled the issue long ago.

But there are a few basic principles that should guide legislators as they tackle comprehensive immigration reform. The solution must reflect the values that have built and sustained America as an immigrant nation. It's about liberty and justice for all.

---

## Chapter Sixteen: THE SOLUTION: Among the sources cited:

U.S. Conference of Catholic Bishops, "Strangers No Longer," April 2004.

Cheryl W. Thompson, The Washington Post, "Obama Vows to Focus on Borders," Aug. 11, 2009.

Pew Hispanic Center, Washington, D.C., "Congressional Debate on Immigration," April 5, 2006.

National Conference of State Legislatures, "Immigrant Policy Project," 2009.

Rick Klein, Boston Globe, "Kennedy, McCain try again on immigration," Feb. 28, 2007.

Coalition for Comprehensive Immigration Reform, "Real Solutions," 2007.

One World.Net, America's Policy Program, "Obama and McCain on immigration," Aug. 19, 2006.

Cam Simpson, The Wall Street Journal, "Obama hones immigration policy," July 21, 2009.

Julia Preston, The New York Times, "Employers fight tough measures on immigration," July 6, 2008.

National Immigration Law Center, Washington, D.C., "Dream Act: Summary," March 2009.

www.ingramcontent.com/pod-product-compliance
Lightning Source LLC
Chambersburg PA
CBHW061400280526
45784CB00001B/319